NOT! THE NINE O'CLOCK NEWS

NOT!

Politics: Five more seats created in House of Commons – so no-one has to sit next to Ian Paisley – Page 68

Profile: A normal Tuesday in Mustique – Page 69

East of England Show: The lovely hopefuls – Page 66

Beauty: Why this woman is suing her Avon Lady – Page 67

Medicine: Britain's latest transplant patient – Page 65

NEWS

Sco~~~~~ found ~~~~~~
'Pay-As-You-Leave' bus

Eco~~~~~
Brit~~~
bu~~~

Im~~~~~
to ~~~~~~~~~
pr~~~~~~

Chicken-pox Spreads
These are now available in Fish and
Marmalade flavours   5

Shoplifting Arab fined for walking
out of Harrods without paying for it   9

SEX   20   s/t

Claire Rayner advises
Don't worry about size, she'll
probably enjoy a good laugh   13

LIVING NOT!   13   s/t

The problems of two-parent families   7

Nuclear power: the alternatives
Do you want to grow two heads and
have your skin drop off in scaly
lumps? Or not?   4

Special survey The 'Which?' report
on hydrogen bombs   5

Medicine
Technicolour man: the first non-racially
prejudiced limb-transplant   4
High Street Sperm Banks: disgusting
new all-night service for women   2

ENTERTAINMENT   22   s/t

TV 4th Channel will exist by 1982:
MPs demand immediate plans for
tunnel underneath it by 1985   23

Sport
Chelsea FC buys first £1m football fan   8

TECHNOLOGY   31   s/t

Destruction of the ozone layer:
is it caused by astronauts
hair-lacquer?   10

Energy
New Tory scheme to help poor
families reduce fuel bills – 'cutting off
their electricity'   2

Motor industry
BL unveil their new mini:
bringing this year's total to 4½   7

PROPERTY   19   s/t

Arabs have stopped buying up large
areas of London: they've got the set   10

JOKE ABOUT FAT PEOPLE   10   s/t

Orson Welles gets on a 'Speak Your
Weight Machine' and the machine
says 'No Coach Parties Please'   3

EXTRAS   3   s/t

Cover charge   18
Inside pages charge   24
Service   16
VAT @ 12½%   19

TOTAL   £1.95

Credit cards not accepted

D0352901

Balmoral every Christmas. Oysters every half hour. Daily Mail every day.

NOT! THE NINE O'CLOCK NEWS

Compiled and Edited by:
Sean Hardie & John Lloyd
Written by (among others)
Clive Anderson, Rowan Atkinson,
Alistair Beaton, Ray Binns,
Colin Bostock Smith, Jeff Blowers,
Arnold Brown, Christopher Burman,
John Cormack, Alan Cubbon, Richard Curtis,
Ian Davidson, Graham Deykin, Kim Fuller,
Colin Gilbert, Andy Hamilton, Sean Hardie,
Jo Harris, David Hewson, Steven Jacobs,
Guy Jenkin, Donnie Kerr, Chris Langham,
Martin Lewis, John Lloyd, Gerald Mahlowe,
Andrew Marshall, Mike Maynard, Chris Miller,
Geoff Nicholson, Karen Osborne, Ray Price,
Nigel Purton, Terry Ravenscroft,
David Renwick, Griff Rhys Jones,
Laurie Rowley, Mel Smith, Richard Sparks,
Pamela Stephenson, Ruby Wax,
Reginald Widdas, Lawrence Windley,
Simon Woodham, (with Douglas Adams).
Picture Research:
Holly Aylett

Photographic Sources:
AEI Cables Ltd, Barnaby's Picture Library, BBC
Central Stills Library, Camera Press Ltd, Chris
Davies, COI, Daily Telegraph, Frank Spooner
Pictures (Gamma), The Guardian, Kentish
Gazette, Keystone Press, Laurie Sparham,
London Express News & Features Services, Mike
Pearce, Popperfoto, Press Association, Radio
Times Hulton Picture Library, Rex Features,
Robert Broeder, Scope Features, Sporting
Pictures (UK) Ltd, The Sun, Syndication
International, The Times, UKAEA, UPI Photo
Library, G Wilson.
Special thanks to bill wilson mike pearce mike
leggo john kilby marcus mortimer mandie
fletcher hillary bevan jones pat ray ros hughes
jenny hunter heather mcgubbin kathy gee
doreen pigram angela lance helen murry daryl
pockett steve connelly paul joel dave hitchcock
marjorie pratt colin lowry colin gilbert hefny
zaki ken major noel chanan dick chamberlain
john treays geoff shaw paul kay mike chislett
jack walsh chris gage dave chapman robin lobb
kezia de winne jackie southern dorinda rea
andrew mackenzie monica boggust nicky rose
harry rankin greg childs jhd gh bw
none of whom have helped type the
manuscript read the text or given the authors
any advice

JL SH   Tehran August 1917

Designed by:
The Small Back Room
with thanks to:
Studio Briggs, Ray Daffurn, Geoff Goode
Photographics, Jo Harris, Longacre,
Karen Osborne, Gary Simmons,
Printed Word.
Additional Artwork:
Steve Connelly, Phil Green, William Hardie,
Daryl Pockett, John Spiers.
Editor:
Sheila Ableman

Published by BBC Books,
an imprint of BBC Worldwide Publishing
BBC Worldwide Ltd, Woodlands,
80 Wood Lane, London W12 0TT

First Published 1980
Reprinted 1980 (four times), 1981 (six times),
1982, 1995
© Not The Nine O'Clock News Ltd 1980
ISBN 0 563 38711 4

Printed in Great Britain by
Butler & Tanner Ltd,
Frome and London

Cover printed by
Richard Clays Ltd, Bungay

NOT!

Letters to the Editor

Dear Alan,

Forgive me for writing to you at the office like this, but I've temporarily lost your address and anyway I'd rather Margaret didn't read what I've got to say. This isn't an easy letter to write, and I only hope that we're old enough friends for you to realise that I only have your interests at heart. I know that in a way you still love Margaret and the kids, and how much effort you've put into saving the marriage. But maybe the two of you should be more honest. Maybe you should tell her about Jenny Giles. And maybe you should know about her and Dick Harrison? (Remember him? Squash player.)

Anyway, read on if it's not too painful.

Tony R.,
The Athaeneum.

Dear Occupant,

Special Offer! Three pence off Coffeemate Economy Size. Offer valid until Dec 30th. Note to retailer: return this voucher to manufacturer who will redeem.

The Occupier,

Anytime. Anywhere. Fullashtray Mini Cabs. Special Wake-the-neighbours-by-mistake Service. 01-2222-8181.

Dear Occupier,

Cisterns of Mercy. Twentyfour-hour pipecleaners. Emergency Services. Nun better!

Personal and Confidential

Dear Alan,

Thanks for coming along to see us last Thursday in connection with the editor's job. The Directors and myself were, of course, impressed by your qualifications – and intrigued by your offer to 'bring over' the contents of the NOT! 'family safe'! However, as you may know, Rees-Evans has now decided to stay on as editor for another couple of years. If you're still interested perhaps we could talk again closer to the time.

Regards, **Peter,**
Thomson Newspapers, London EC1

Dear Mr Editor,

I'm pleased to be able to tell you that you, Mr Edotir, have been personally selected from among literally thousands of householders to take part in our unique Win An Ocean Liner Contest. Entry is absolute free when you agree to add the Oditer family to family to the list of millions of satisfied subscribers to the Collectors' Edition of Vintage Yellow Pages. These volumes, originally published by the Post Office in 1973, are agreed by experts to be of outstanding rarity. Every month you'll receive an additional hand-posted page, building over the years into a complete Classified Directory. Page one covers Abbatoir Equipment to Accommodation Address Agents. Page two Accountants. And so on. Apply within seven days and we'll also send you absolutely free a facsimile 1965 STD Code Book.

Without obligation. See envelope for details.

World Leisure Ltd,
PO Box 94, Swindon 8

Saudi Arabia: An Apology

It has been drawn to our attention that certain references in recent issues of this magazine could be constructed as implying some criticism of the peoples and culture of the Kingdom of Saudi Arabia.

We welcome this opportunity to withdraw unreservedly any such implications, and can assure Saudi readers that they will under no circumstances be repeated in this and future issues. We feel that you're a wonderful people with big hearts, a rich and varied culture, and an awful lot of oil, and if you like we'll happily lie down and let you walk up and down all over us. Any time.

And if you want to kill princesses, that's fine by us. You could even have one of ours, if you want. Two maybe.

We think you're a warm, wonderful, wealthy people, and that we in Britain would be a damn sight better off if we had a good strict system of morality like you do. The trouble is we can't afford to because if we did then rich Arabs wouldn't want to come over here to gamble and screw and get pissed.

Dear Sir,

I notice from your account that you are now 576 lb 9 oz overdrawn.

Please telephone me to arrange an early appointment to discuss repayment.

Yours faithfully, **C. Giles,**
Deputy Manager, Barclays Sperm Bank, Monmouth Road, W2

Dear Dad,

I hope you are well. Thanks for sending me the pen, which is great. I'd like a Casio Biorythm Stopwatch Radio for my birthday – you can get them from that mail order place that advertises in one of the colour supplements. Yesterday we were meant to play Stowe (I'm still touch-judge) but their team are still in san with Legionnaires' Disease – so it was called off.

I'm writing this during prep – Bongles has set an essay about the break-up of the nuclear family and I'm doing it about you and Mummy.

Love from **Justin,**
Uppingham College, Leics.

P.S. Tony R has written a very strange letter.

Dear Alan,

If that's the way you treat your secretaries, then stuff it. I'm off. I suppose it's my own stupid fault for trusting you in the first place – only now do I realise that our relationship meant absolutely nothing to you. Not that it matters now – since Jenny and I have decided to get married after all.

Yours, **Hilary**

P.S. I haven't touched your mail. Doubtless it won't take you long to find some empty-headed little temp to deal with it.

Letters do not necessarily represent the views of the Editor of NOT! but frankly stand precious little chance of getting published otherwise.

The Editor reserves the right to shorten letters for reasons of spa

BRITAIN'S APPLICATION TO JOIN THE THIRD WORLD TURNED DOWN

Mrs Thatcher receives news of the latest unemployment figures

The Queen's Speech

My government does not intend to shirk its responsibilities in the coming months. The most pressing of these is unemployment. Legislation will be introduced before the Christmas recess to place the jobless on exercise bicycles whose dynamos can be harnessed to the National Grid. This should both keep them fit for World War Three and solve the energy crisis. It will also provide a welcome boost for our ailing Exercise Bicycle Industry. Later in the year a Green Paper will be published setting out proposals to melt down all unemployed persons living in the vicinity of main roads to extract their lead content for export.

Secondly, the Environment. The Prime Minister is determined that the Third London Airport will definitely be built at Stansted – and next time she really means it. To alleviate the objections of ecologists, it is proposed that every deaf person in the country will be moved to the Stanstead area, and the present occupants rehoused in a really quiet place like Maplin Sands.

The Leader of the House will take steps to tackle the problem of dung-throwing from the public galleries. His office intend to contact EQUUS, the horses' union, with a proposal that they voluntarily restrict their lobbying to six pickets. That is all for the moment.

The Buck Starts Here

UNEMPLOYMENT
Black Economy

Mrs Thatcher has ordered an immediate inquiry into the number of jobless blacks. She feels there aren't enough.

NORTHERN IRELAND
Rhyme Squad

The Provisional IRA have admitted responsibility for the Irish Entry in the Eurovision Song Contest.

ENTERTAINMENT
Crash Bang Wallop

Since the split-up of Peters and Lee, Lee has gone solo and Peters has gone straight into a lamp-post.

CRIME
Scots on The Rocks

Six Scotsmen arrested last week in Saudi Arabia returned home today. They were accused of drinking alcohol, but released after the Saudi Justice Minister explained that his country respected the religions of other nations.

TELECOMMUNICATIONS
Stick Up

The GPO are to issue a new series of stamps honouring famous British Novelists. The 10p has scenes from *Wuthering Heights,* the 12½p depicts *Jane Eyre* and the £18.50 shows scenes from *Confessions Of A Window Cleaner.*

DEFENCE
Bang On Time

British Pentagon-watchers at the World Strategic Defence Institute have analysed the reason for the current behaviour of the USA. They believe that the Americans are trying to make up for the fact that they were late for the last two World Wars by being really punctual this time.

TRANSPORT
Carriage Cock

Mr Norman Fowler, the Transport Minister who has vowed to improve British Rail, arrived by train today in Kowloon, China, the first stop on his fact-finding tour of Scotland.

TRAVEL
Wide Bodied

Lord Goodman boarded a Jumbo Jet yesterday for an early Christmas break in the South of France. The plane was last seen on the M62 heading towards Dover.

INFLATION
Worst Class

First-class stamps are to go up to 15p from next week. That's 2p for postage and 13p for storage.

Country Diary

Windscale Thurs.

The mild spring, a long wet summer, and the usual autumn leak from the storage tanks behind B generator have forced many species to mutate early this year. Walking up Haile Fell on a damp October morning last week-end I spotted no fewer than seventeen tri-ped Herdwick tups – once a rarity in these parts. There have also been reports of a family of pterodactyls nesting in the cliffs above Ennerdale Lake, to the irritation of some shepherds. I strolled up the shore on Monday in the hope of sighting one, but had to content myself with a brace of giant headless grebe feeding off two Friends of the Earth behind the reprocessor plant. Fishermen are having difficulty catching kippers off the marine overflow pipes – here's hoping for an early shipment of Japanese uranium once the winter storms get going in earnest!

SH

RIGHT: Doctors' concern about the new fertility drug Sixbrat-90, and its possible side-effects, was successfully allayed after Mrs E Hawkins (right) successfully gave birth to a pair of pyjamas at Guys Hospital on Monday.

BELOW: The GPO unveil TOM, their new Speaking Cock Service.

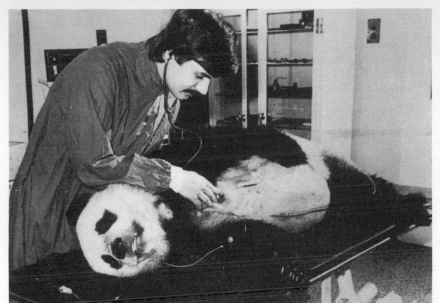

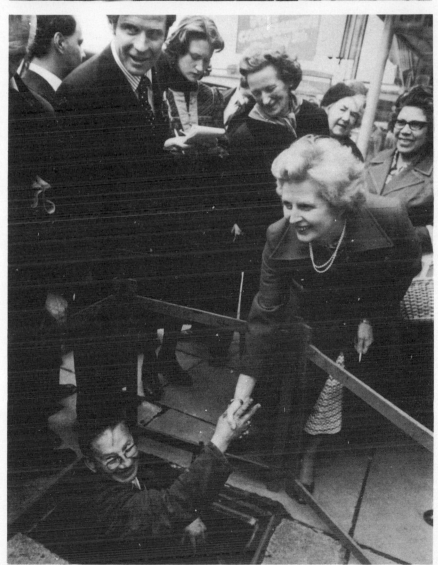

RIGHT: Mrs Thatcher opens the prestigious new Glasgow Underground.

ABOVE: A member of the Windscale Swimming Club returns glowing from a quick dip.

In-flight catering
A MAN-SIZED MEAL
The last flight of DAG 4567

On 10 August 1979 a Dago-Air jumbo jet, flight DAG 4567, from Palma, Majorca, disappeared without trace on a routine flight to Chicago. Speculation as to the cause of the crash was intense and wide-ranging.

Three main theories, however, emerged:
1 The Iraqi ground-crew at Sangria International Airport had neglected to replace the tail-section after dismantling it for cleaning.
2 Insufficient fuel was placed in the tanks by the charter company, who were in the habit of admixing the kerosene with three parts in a hundred of lucozade.
3 A dispute broke out between plain-clothes FBI sky-marshals and armed Israeli security guards who were discussing the merits of Barbra Streisand's performance in the in-flight movie, which culminated in a prolonged gunfight two hundred miles south of Greenland.

No trace, however, of either the plane, its passengers or crew, was ever found – until three weeks ago, when two sole survivors of the disaster staggered, barely able to stand, from the smoking remains of their lonely ten-month barbecue in the Adirondack Mountains of Canada.

NOT! has obtained their exclusive story.

Survivor 1: The lights came on . . . 'No Smoking' . . . 'Fasten Safety Belts'. Then everything just dropped.

Survivor 2: I blacked out. When I came to . . . the cold . . . that was the first thing I noticed. The cold.

NOT!: I see. Now it was . . . three weeks, wasn't it, before you decided . . .

Survivor 2: Yes.

> It remains a mystery to me why manufacturers cannot make their aircraft out of the same stuff they use to make their black box flight recorders . . .
> **Board of Trade Investigator's Report**

Survivor 1: We . . . put it off for as long as we could.

Survivor 2: But of course . . . f . . . fu . . . food . . . was essential.

Survivor 1: I mean . . . we had several meetings. And if it hadn't been a unanimous vote . . .

NOT!: And who . . . who took the lead, if that isn't an unfair question?

Survivor 2: Oh all of us.

Survivor 1: But mainly me. I was the hungriest.

NOT!: So, when you'd all agreed?

Survivor 1: I went back into the aeroplane. I went inside. I'll never forget it. It was sort of unreal. But I was numbed . . . you know?

NOT!: I believe you . . . prayed?

Survivor 2: We all did. Before . . . before . . .

Survivor 1: Yes. We all said grace. It seemed the least we could do.

NOT!: Please go on, if it's not too painful.

Survivor 1: So . . . I had a pocket knife. And I went in. And, I, I brought *some* back.

NOT!: And what did you eat first?

Survivor 1: I . . . I don't remember.

Survivor 2: The gherkins.

Survivor 1: That's right . . . it was the gherkins.

Survivor 2: Then the individual cheese portions, then the folded piece of ham . . . which was still . . . glistening . . . and still had the . . . little slice of pear on top. And finally, O God, the . . . puddings.

NOT!: And how did you feel after you'd eaten the airline food?

Survivor 2: Awful. Awful. But as we said . . . it was our only chance.

Survivor 1: Yes, I mean we'd already eaten all the passengers.

NOT!: Thank you.

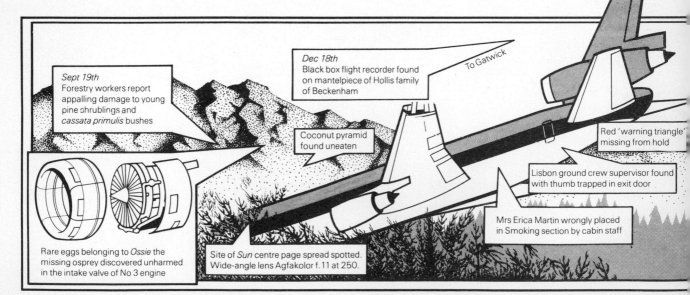

Sept 19th
Forestry workers report appalling damage to young pine shrublings and *cassata primulis* bushes

Dec 18th
Black box flight recorder found on mantelpiece of Hollis family of Beckenham

To Gatwick

Coconut pyramid found uneaten

Red 'warning triangle' missing from hold

Lisbon ground crew supervisor found with thumb trapped in exit door

Mrs Erica Martin wrongly placed in Smoking section by cabin staff

Rare eggs belonging to *Ossie* the missing osprey discovered unharmed in the intake valve of No 3 engine

Site of *Sun* centre page spread spotted. Wide-angle lens Agfakolor f.11 at 250.

Menu

Marrowskin Segments in Brine

or

First Officer Harold Willis

Cerveaux du Chat Irlandais
Chunky portions of Limerick kitten on wet toast

or

Pierre duGarde
A computer export sales manager from Rouen, France

Cocktail Sausages Façon de Qantas
Served in a thin film of polywrap

or

Anne-Marie Spencer-Jones
An airline hostess from Croydon, Surrey

Salade Cousteau
Shredded Italian seaweed on a bed of cabbage

or

Mrs Karl Schmidt
Housewife from Düsseldorf, West Germany

Creme Sago

or

Cardinal Alberto Compostella
Papal delegate to Chile

Ryvita, Primula

or

David Cohen
Airline security officer, Natanyn, Israel

Polo Mints

Coffeemate

or

Something in a Plastic Bag We Can't Put A Name To

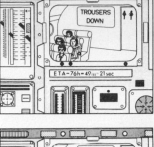

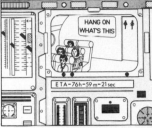

The new McDonnell Douglas Maximum-Security Water-Closet. A laser-guided electronic beam eye inside the cubicle is connected to the exterior display panel, allowing the cabin crew at a glance to check on movements of occupant. Pictures above show how a typical sequence appears on the co-pilot's closed-circuit TV monitor on the flight-deck.

Under new safety regulations, leading airlines have withdrawn all aircraft over sixteen years old and put them out to stud.

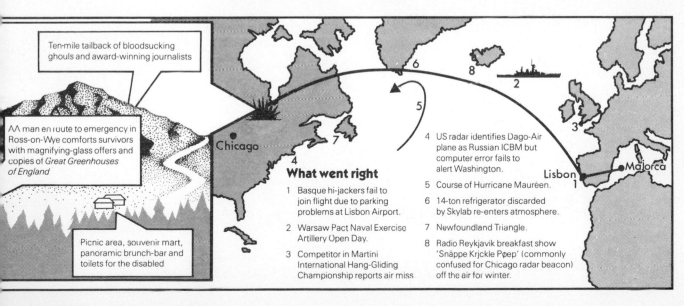

Ten-mile tailback of bloodsucking ghouls and award-winning journalists

AA man en route to emergency in Ross-on-Wye comforts survivors with magnifying-glass offers and copies of *Great Greenhouses of England*

Picnic area, souvenir mart, panoramic brunch-bar and toilets for the disabled

What went right

1 Basque hi-jackers fail to join flight due to parking problems at Lisbon Airport.

2 Warsaw Pact Naval Exercise Artillery Open Day.

3 Competitor in Martini International Hang-Gliding Championship reports air miss

4 US radar identifies Dago-Air plane as Russian ICBM but computer error fails to alert Washington.

5 Course of Hurricane Maureen.

6 14-ton refrigerator discarded by Skylab re-enters atmosphere.

7 Newfoundland Triangle.

8 Radio Reykjavik breakfast show 'Snäppe Krjckle Pøep' (commonly confused for Chicago radar beacon) off the air for winter.

Chicago

Lisbon

Majorca

You can taste a hop in Schlössmeister

Here at Schlössmeister Breweries we've been making Lager since 1979. And we brew it the way only Germans appreciate.

We've combined the timeless taste of the Volkswagen. The flavour of pre-war Hamburg. The finest Düsseldorf tap-water. Specially selected by-products from the chemical industries of the Ruhr. Then we leave it overnight in a plastic vat. Inject it with carbon monoxide. Stick a picture of Lichtenstein on the label.

And ship it direct to your supermarket. In handy aerosol packs.

Schlössmeister Lager

Archibald Schlössmeister & Son,
The Carpet Works, Daventry

– as German as Cricket itself

 (label on bottle: Schlössmeister Lager, 275ml 9.68 floz, BREWED DAVE)

MISSION INEFFABLE

The diary of a stunt pope

It's 6.48 a.m. and Syd Heslop is getting ready for work. A quick shave, a light breakfast, twenty press-ups, and just time left to answer a call of nature and glance through the *Daily Star* City Page.

Nothing extraordinary about that.

Except that Syd's is no ordinary job.

For Syd Heslop is a special breed: one of a small band of men who every day put their own safety at risk. Ten minutes later, pausing only to slip on his vestments, Syd runs into the street, plunging head first through a two-inch teak door, and lands genuflecting on one knee: his left hand holding a gold-embossed crozier while his right executes a flawless gesture of beatification.

For Syd Heslop is a Stunt Pope.

One of a select group of some 45 Papal Stand-ins who operate all over the world, thus enabling His Holiness to be internationally Omnipresent.

7.00 am. Just routine. Another day begins for a stunt pope.

"Basically it all started when JP got worried about the papal image," says Syd, who's 49 and comes from Basildon in Essex. "Especially after the last two popped off so sudden, like, it began to look as if the Roman Candles had lost the celestial nod. So he decided to put it about, go for the all-action bit. And of course one man can only do so much . . ."

5.30 pm. Embarrassing moment. Syd meets the real thing outside a launderette in Bologna.

In the past two years, Syd's work has taken him all over the world – Mexico, Brazil, even Poland.

"Generally speaking I step in for any risky stuff: waving from high balconies, visiting Ireland, blessing the contagiously sick and so on."

Physical fitness is essential, the training punishing.

"Every day begins with roadwork. I try and tone up the muscles essential to any world-class religious leader. Normally I do ten miles, or "decem" as we call them in the trade, and end up with two hundred genuflections – a hundred on the right knee, then a hundred on the left. This helps keep my mortal coil tuned to a high pitch of perfection."

Syd (left) meets the Archbishop of York.

And there are the stunts, which John Paul tends to delegate for insurance reasons. Syd is currently practising a motorcycle jump from the balcony of St Peter's.

"I hope to clear twenty thousand American pilgrims and land on the Tiber Expressway. Balancing the incense holders at that height is absolute hell."

In Rome, the Vatican is reluctant to talk about Syd and his colleagues. A Curia spokesman insists that Pope John Paul does all his own stunts:

"Of course he does. For example next week he intends to reaffirm the doctrine of Papal Infallibility by performing a freefall drop from 40,000 feet, without a parachute." He added that it might be dangerous for children to try to imitate His Holiness.

And it's not exactly child's play for Syd, either.

"Well, basically, plummeting 40,000 feet to certain death is going to require split-second timing. Still, at least when a stunt Pope snuffs it they keep you on the payroll. Then when His Holiness pops off he can lie in state in several places at once."

Syd's big moment: 40,000 feet free fall without a parachute.

Syd practises his judo-holds on the Bishop of Montevideo.

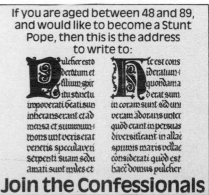

This page has been left blank
in order to try and attract
readers of the Daily Express.

CHURCH UNITY: A NEW INITIATIVE

The Devil – Is he all bad?

The liberalisation of the Anglican Church has, in recent years, provoked a fundamental reassessment of the rôle of minority groups inside the Church of England.

Today, Methodists, Gays – even Stouts – are freely accepted into the Anglican Communion.

And church-goers are calling for the reversal of Lambeth's traditional hostility towards another Old Enemy: The Devil. They are led by the Rev Terry Mountjoy, an Anglican priest who sympathises with the plight of diabolists – devil-worshippers who find it difficult to gain acceptance in a Christian world.

"Well, ya. Personally, I feel that in a sense, the Devil has had a very poor press," Mountjoy affirms. "After all, what do we really *mean* by 'bad'? I mean, look, come on. This is Wandsworth. You know? No, really, I feel that modern Christians should show a bit less of the 'Get thee behind me, Satan!', and a bit more of the 'Come on in, old mate, have a cup of tea'."

Virgin boeuf

So what sort of people are present-day diabolists? George and Fiona Timmis live in an elegant Gothic penthouse with an excellent view of London's Smithfield Market. George is 42, and a steward with British Airways.

"We don't have any problems, really," he says.

"Well," interjects his wife, "maybe the murdering . . ."

"Well, yes, except for the murdering. That can be a problem. I mean if you get an exceptionally difficult goat, well, then obviously, it can make a noise. But, you see, these days we diabolists, we're not your sort of 'mumbo-jumbo' Denis Wheatley types.

George and Fiona ravish each other till dawn

The Rev Terry Mountjoy (centre) greets parishioners after Matins

Not at all. It's much more modern, more up-to-date."

"Coffee mornings, bring-and-buy sales . . ."

Bring-and-buy sales?

"Well . . . I *say* bring-and-buy sales," George reflects, "but it's more sort of murdering *actually*. You know, rape . . ."

"Virgins," murmurs Fiona.

"Virgins," agrees George. "Oxen. Coffee. Of a morning."

Bread and Buddha

The Rev Mountjoy's response is thoughtful.

"Virgins? What's a virgin? I mean, *I've* never met one," he quips. "No, seriously, I think it's something we'd be prepared to have a natter about. And, yes. Ya. Yup. Cautiously, I think I would approve of slaughtering the odd virgin. Fair enough."

But mere murder is not the whole of the devil-worshippers' creed. Fiona Timmis: "We believe that Satan, Prince of Darkness, is Lord of the Universe and will destroy Jesus through infernal power."

Mountjoy admits this is a difficult one. "It's tricky, obviously. It's one of those 'theological grey areas'. But I believe we should keep a broad outlook. After all, intrinsically all religions have the same root. I mean, Christianity is basically no different from Buddhism. Similarly, Moslems are just like Christians, only with more money."

Pope springs eternal

Nevertheless, fundamental similarities aside, forms of worship differ, as George Timmis explains. "Every full moon we do go up to the Heath at midnight, then we do strip naked and ravish each other passionately until the dawn." Which helps them summon up the forces of Evil? George says categorically: "Who cares?"

Human Sacrifice – ". . . it's much more up to date these days . . ."

Terry Mountjoy is optimistic about the possibility of accepting people like George and Fiona into the Church.

"Bound to happen. I personally think it's only a matter of time before diabolists are accepted into the *priesthood*. Of course, some people will oppose it. The Pope, I think, is probably anti. But it's on the cards. Definitely."

On the question of whether diabolists would welcome an invitation to join the Church of England, Fiona Timmis is enigmatic. "I couldn't give a toss," she says.

News in brief

NEAR EAST
Bottoms Up
Jeddah: in his new budget announced today, the Chancellor of Saudi Arabia has put twenty lashes on a bottle of whisky.

AFRICA
Banana Bunch
In a joint communiqué issued yesterday in Salisbury, Rev. Canaan Banana has denied allegations of nepotism amongst his cabinet. The statement was co-signed by Cardinal Moses Pineapple, His Eminence Ndabaningi Toffee Apple, and the Prime Minister, Mr Robert Rhubarbe.

CENTRAL AMERICA
Ass Liquor
Puerto Rican police have confirmed that the main turbine failure which brought the island to a standstill over the weekend was the work of saboteurs. Allegedly, traces of Horlicks have been found in the donkey.

VATICAN
Papal Pull
Next year's prospective Italian entry to the Eurovision Song Contest, *I Can't Get No Contraception,* has been cancelled after the Pope advised them to pull out at the last minute.

AFRICA
For Love Of Lybia
Unconfirmed sources in Tripoli report that Colonel Gaddafi of Libya has survived another assassination attempt. Doctors say the bullet went right through the middle of his head and missed his brain by six feet.

EUROPE
Schmidt Phase
The West German Chancellor, Herr Schmidt, today announced measures designed to bring full employment to Europe, create closer ties between the allies, and provide a welcome slap in the face for Russian expansionism. He has invaded Czechoslovakia.

USA
Dental Cheque
In the legal proceedings surrounding the Osmonds' split-up, Donny Osmond has been awarded custody of the teeth.

SOUTH AFRICA
Drown Draft
In measures designed to further relax the apartheid laws, Mr Botha has introduced South Africa's first racially mixed swimming pool. The whites get the top half, and the blacks get the bottom half.

COMMON MARKET
The EEC Budget: How It Works
Extract from the Official Transcript of Ministerial Question Time at last week's European Parliamentary Sessions.

Rear-Admiral Sir Gervase Hibbert (Conservative, Dorking (Golf Course)): Will the Minister comment on the latest figures for budgetary contributions by member countries of the EEC?

M. Brochure d'Esplanade, EEC Foreign Minister: Certainly. The question being asked by you and back home in your country, Britain, is this: are the sizes of these donations fair? The answer, I will tell you straight, is no.

Why should this be so, you ask? Well, if you were to think about it, the answer would be obvious. The British are paying more to the EEC because everyone else in the EEC hates Britain, that's why. Why must you always be looking for complex economic answers? We want to bleed your crummy little island till it dies of anaemia.

Don't think for one moment we've forgotten Agincourt! Oh, no. Or the Battle of Waterloo, or the mess you made of our beaches in Normandy, or Sandie Shaw winning the Eurovision Song Contest. We hate your puppet on a string, and we're going to make you pay for it all Mr Smith, Mr Jones and Mr Robinson. We hate your lamb, we hate your Cox's Pippins, we hate your Mini car. Don't you realise how much we loathe your David Niven, and your Inspector Clouseau – I would like a rheum, oh yes, very funny, ha ha ha ha. Well, the laugh's on you this time, mate. We hate your 'mate', we hate your 'old boy', your 'good chap', your false camaraderie and your false teeth, your humeur anglaise, your Shakespeare and your Boomtown Rats. We don't need your raison d'être, so up your cul de sac with your je ne sais quoi...

EEC Budget: Who pays?

Member country	Contribution (Sterling)	Contribution (Members' own currency)
Denmark	£1.2 million	2.4 million kroners
Holland	£1.6 million	3.7 million guilders
Belgium	£0.9 million	2.4 million benders
Ireland	2 hats	5 hats
Germany	£4.0 million	8.8 million marks
France	38p	4.2 francs
Italy	£1.0 million*	8,908,785,344,325.68 billion grubby little coloured rags
Luxembourg	1 evening with Princess Astrid	2.4 bangs
United Kingdom	£4,000 million	£4,000 million (plus VAT)

*plus four tons of quick-mix cannelloni

HYANNISPORT, USA: Auditions being held for Senator Edward Kennedy's new chauffeur.

IRAQ: Platoon of Iraqi cavalry cross the Iranian border, mounted on inflatable Arianna Stassinopoulos dolls.

ZIMBABWE: Joshua Nkomo gained three more seats in the Zimbabwe National Parliament on Thursday, when he sat on Bishop Muzorewa and two of his supporters.

Ladies and gentlemen, Captain Wang and his crew welcome you aboard Flight 12.03 to Los Angeles. We hope that you will have a pleasant flight and that we do not encounter any turbulence and crash the plane. For your own safety and convenience, please locate the instruction card in the pouch in front of you. It is situated in between the crumpled magazine with the Robert Morley interview, and the piece of orange peel. We would like to stress that in the unlikely event of anything going wrong any attempt to escape from the aircraft is futile. Please fasten your safety belt and extinguish your cigarette. Shame though it is to waste your last one. When disaster strikes, there may be a slight loss of cabin pressure and a reduction in the number of wings. In this event, a plastic mask will drop down automatically. Place it over your nose, and pull hard to release the oxygen. Then attempt to fil the broken cord back into the hole from which the air is now pouring. Please note that your lifejacket is under your seat. It is impossible to get the jacket out particularly with your seat belt on, so we have one already prepared here. Place it over the head. Then tie the straps around you. To inflate, pull the yellow tag, press the green button, unzip the toggle pocket, unscrew the air valve anti-clockwise and yell 'inflate you stupid bugger'. Next remove from your person any sharp objects, such as fragments of red-hot engine-casing, and make your way to the escape routes. These are located over the wings so you people, there, there, and there have absolutely no chance and we apologise for having wasted your time. Well, enough of this maudlin talk, this has been your chief stewardess speaking. Demonstrating the regulations was Lola, who's a right little strumpet and willing to oblige you in any way at all when or if we reach Madrid. Captain Wang and his crew wish you a very short journey and pleasant flight. Thank you.

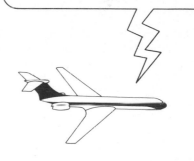

DAGO-AIR

– almost
as safe as
sword-swallowing

Soldier of Fortune!

It's a job with a future. You get security. Good money. The grub's great. You'll meet new people. Develop new skills. You can learn to shoot, to drive a tank – even to fly.

The sporting opportunities are unrivalled. Sailing, water-skiing, wind-surfing.

And you'll travel all over the world – at our expense.

And if you think it's all peeling spuds and cleaning your boots, you couldn't be more wrong.

Join The Royal Family

– you'll find us in the Almanac de Gotha under W

Shoppers Guide
to the
Best Cuts of Alligator

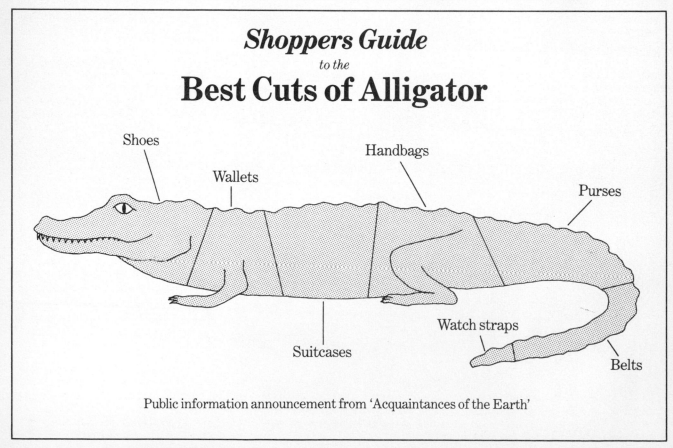

Shoes

Wallets

Handbags

Purses

Suitcases

Watch straps

Belts

Public information announcement from 'Acquaintances of the Earth'

The James Burke Column

Good morning. Or *is* it? This week I'm going to ask the very important questions: Who do I think I am? What am I doing? What the hell am I talking about? And why do I keep appearing on television performing mindless visual tricks when Paul Daniels does it so much better?

Isn't it something to do with the fact that I have to constantly question the last thing I just said. Or *is* it? Or *isn't* it? Or is *or* isn't it?

Well, it can all be summed up in one sentence. So why isn't it? You see what I mean? No? Good.

Because the basic idea of all this manic behaviour and meaningful stares can be put into five words: "I'm Clever, But You're Stupid".

And that's the reason why I can do this sort of thing on television at peak viewing time, because if you did it you'd be locked up.

Get it? No? Excellent.

So there we have it. The truth of the theory is really very, very simple. And if it isn't, I change it so it is. Or do I?

COVER STORY

YES

TO MR & MRS KIRTNALL

The following letter from JOHN KIRTNALL, the kidnapped London schoolboy, was delivered to the office of NOT! by his captors who believe his parents to be readers of this magazine. If they are, could they please contact the Editor's secretary during normal office hours.

Tuesday 13th

Dear Mum and Dad,
I'm afraid this isn't a very easy letter to write. I'm all right. Don't panic – everything seems to be all right. Mum in particular, don't panic. If you feel yourself starting to panic for heavens sake take the pill or something to calm you down.

no milk? Well this guy does it just that way, but he puts in a lot of pepper and something else just to add tast. (He's telling me its parsley). Then at lunch we

The thing is, I've been kidnapped, but I'm sure it will be all right. They've been very good to me so far. This morning for breakfast we had scrambled eggs, which were really good. You know that way of making them with just eggs, no milk? Well this guy goes it just that way, but he puts in a lot of pepper and something else just to add taste. (He's telling me it's parsley).

really tangy tast, made with some kind of hot pepper sauce and tuna fish and rice, and I think there was some sweet-corn in there somewhere – anyway, it was Great.

Then at lunch we had kipper paté. No, sorry, he says it was smoked mackerel. Anyway whatever it was, it was really great and after it we had this sort of paella, but this really tangy taste, made with some kinds of hot pepper sauce and tuna fish and rice, and I think there was some sweetcorn in there somewhere – anyway, it was great.

So the point is, everything is just fine – don't panic. I'm eating well, really well, and there seems to be no reason to suspect that the standard of meals is going to drop.

So the point is, everything is just fine – don't panic. I'm eating well, really well, and there seems to be no reason to suspect that the standard of meals is going to drop.

Anyway, to get to the point, the fact is this. They want forty million quid. I know it's a lot to ask, particularly since they're such a small outfit (just two of them, John and Peter) – but they're great guys and they say that if you don't pay the money they'll have to kill me. I think it's tomorrow. (Peter's just come in and he says yes, it is tomorrow). So please Mum and Dad, pay up.

and so on. So they would appreciate it is you could just send the money to: JOHN and PETER ROGERS, 13, MONMOUTH GROVE, LONDON. W13. And please send it first class because I feel I'm a bit of an

Two last things. I want you to know that when I've finished this message I'm going to have tea, which is already on, and looks like being great. Crumpets and some kind of home-made jam, so don't worry about me. The other thing is, they say they can't be doing with all this complicated handover stuff because there's a lot of shopping to be done and pre-cooking for Christmas and so on. So they would appreciate it if you could just send the money to:
John and Peter Rogers,
13, Monmouth Grove,
London W13.

And please send it first class because I feel I'm a bit of an imposition here, eating them out of house and home etc. Also of course if it doesn't get here by first post on Monday (the day after tomorrow) I cop it.

> *love*
> *John.*

The above insertion was held over from last week's issue due to unofficial industrial action. We extend our sincerest apologies to Mr and Mrs Kirtnall, and apologise for any inconvenience caused.

TORY CONFERENCE

The Young Turks' Delight

Despite rare murmurings of dissent (see picture) Conference this year was largely distinguished by the fiery 'no U-turns' oratory of the new breed of Tory.

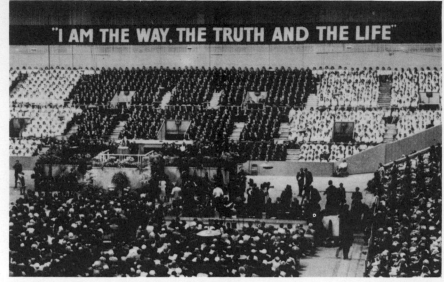

Mrs Thatcher in confident mood at Brighton.

Lower middle-class, self-made, with a fat tie and expensive Italian shoes, John Radcliffe, a delegate from Hunslett, is typical of the mould. His speech follows below.

"Our Right Honourable Leader – and Denis…my Lords and Ladies…fellow Party workers. I am a golfer. (APPLAUSE) And I am also a Conservative. And the Conservatives are in *power,* what a wonderful word! But with a new initiative, and most importantly a new style. Because there is an image – isn't there? – of the Conservative as a sort of fuddy-duddy, middle-aged, middle-class, sort of 'fascist' type, which is clearly such rubbish as to be hardly worth talking about.

Sir Geoffrey Howe, Chancellor of the Exchequer, said he was delighted with the latest inflation figure of 16¾ per cent, as it's 12 per cent less than at the same time next year.

Obviously, there are a few of these people about, whom I think would be better off *shot* (LAUGHTER) . . . but most of us are jolly reasonable, intelligent people who *just happen to hate bloody socialists!* (APPLAUSE)

We are still mostly concerned with two main issues. Firstly, immigration. Now people really do get this party wrong every time on this issue. We think immigration ought to be curbed: O.K. But we don't think immigrants are *animals,* for God's sake! I know a lot of immigrants. Personally. And they're perfectly nice people. They're black, of course – which is a shame – but, honestly, some of them can do some jobs almost as well as English people. And we acknowledge this. But having said that, all we would ask is this: do we really *need* them? Couldn't we just *do without* them? Now a lot of immigrants are Indians and Pakistanis, for instance. And I *like* curry. I do.

Mrs Thatcher told a jubilant Conference that she could not send food and supplies to war-torn Ethiopia as Harrods don't deliver that far.

But now that we've *got* the recipes, if you like, is there really any need for them to stay?

Conservatives understand these problems. As we understand the problem of young criminals – another very emotive issue. This party feels that we've been just a little bit too soft on these . . . *bastards,* for want of a better word.

Now, one must be reasonable, of course. Compassionate certainly. But we do think that just a little tightening up of discipline could go a long way. Mr Whitelaw has spoken of the 'short sharp shock' treatment, and his introduction of the electric chair to two Home Office detention centres over the last eleven months, on a purely experimental basis of course, may sound harsh. It *is* harsh. But as a party we are convinced that this has gone a long way to reducing the number of young offenders in

---

Energy Minister Michael Heseltine told Conference that, in order to bring it into line with other domestic heating fuels, the Government would shortly be announcing a 45 per cent increase in the price of furniture.

---

our detention centres. The new Conservatism works. If it doesn't, then of course, we will be more than happy to revert to the old liberal, wishy-washy, nigger-loving, socialist, red, left-wing, homosexual, commie ways of the recent past.

But, please, let us have the chance. It may be a tough road yet a while, but don't forget, 'It is easier for a rich man to pass through the eye of a needle, than it is for a camel to . . . ah . . . than it is for a camel to!' Thank you." (APPLAUSE)

Mr Callaghan finds a new position for Tony Benn.

TORY CONFERENCE

LIBERAL CONFERENCE

Sir Keith Joseph Brings In New Top Men For Industry

At a total cost believed to be in the region of £9,000 million a year, Industry Secretary Sir Keith Joseph has brought in ten new experts from the private sector to fill Britain's top jobs in National Corporations, he announced to Conference yesterday. The new brooms are:

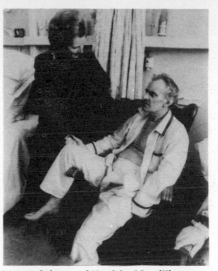
New Minister of Health. £3 million.

David Steel Says Liberals Need A Lift

Liberal Leader David Steel told cheering party workers that they badly needed a lift, they deserved a lift, and by next year they would have a lift. They would hold the Party Conference in it, he promised. The massive new popularity of the Liberals had made this year's telephone kiosk far too crowded.

Liberal Policy, he said, rested on two vital new planks. Firstly, they had to find out whether or not the Labour Party still existed, and secondly, urgent research must be done into finding a new nightie for official wear at Party parties. Conference passed both resolutions unanimously.

New Minister for Agriculture and Fisheries. £4 million.

New First Sea Lord. £5 million for a short time.

New Chairman of Milk Marketing Board. £9 million.

Sir Ranulph Twistleton-Wykeham-Fiennes' trans-world expedition to find out whether the Labour Party still exists.

Five New Police Commissioners. £3 million each.

New Chairman of IBA. £7 million.

Liberal Peers test a new nightgown for Party parties.

"I want a lot more monkey ie 500lb"

Gerald at the microphone being interviewed by a reporter from the 'Canberra Herald' for a feature on road safety. (Arrant bosh. (a) Bear again; (b) Lollipop, not microphone. Picture editor to my office at once—Ed).

In the past few years there have been some extraordinary breakthroughs in communication between men and animals, some outstanding cases being those with dolphins and with owls.

In the forefront of this field is Professor Timothy Fielding, and his experiments with a gorilla called Gerald. Pamela Stephenson went to see them:

Extracts:

STEPHENSON: Professor, can Gerald really speak, as we would understand it?

PROFESSOR: Oh yes, yes. He can speak a few actual words. But it was an enormously difficult task even to get him to this stage. I mean, when I first captured Gerald in the Congo, er...in '67 I think it was...

GERALD: '68.

PROFESSOR: '68...there were years of work ahead. At first he was enormously slow and difficult, and I had to put in a vast amount of time. I worked constantly on him...

GERALD: Look, if I could just butt in here a moment, Tim, I have done a considerable amount of work on this project myself. And to be frank, your teaching style leaves a lot to...

PROFESSOR: That's a bit ungrateful isn't it?

GERALD: And your diction isn't really up to...

PROFESSOR: Now, look. Let me put this in perspective. When I *caught* Gerald in '68, he was completely *wild*...

Among his many accomplishments, Gerald lists being Television Critic of the 'Daily Star'. (Is it just me, or isn't that a bear rather than a gorilla?—Ed).

GERALD: Wild? I was livid! Never been treated like such a twat in my life!

STEPHENSON: But...ah...that's all changed now hasn't it? Because, Professor, you've since actually brought Gerald up in your own home...

PROFESSOR: Yes, yes, he actually lives with me.

GERALD: Though not in the "biblical" sense, of course!

Gerald and his constant companion, actress Suzette Timpani. (It is a bear, dammit. And who's 'Suzette Timpani'? Sounds like a made-up name to me.—Ed).

STEPHENSON: And does he miss... er...do you miss having a mate, Gerald?

GERALD: Oh no! I've got lots of mates. The Professor, his son Toby, Raymond next door...Oh. Oh I see what you mean! Crumpet!

STEPHENSON: Yes, well, that was in fact what...

PROFESSOR: You didn't tell me you were friendly with Raymond.

GERALD: Well, do I have to tell you *everything?*

PROFESSOR: Anyway, after about nine years, we really began to get somewhere, and...

GERALD: That reminds me actually. I was just pointing out to the Professor the other day, you know how you tell jokes about the Irish not being very clever? Americans and "Polack" jokes and so on? Well, back home we have the same sort of jokes, only about orang-utangs—who aren't famous for being all that bright.

STEPHENSON: Really, how fascinating.

PROFESSOR: I've heard this one.

GERALD: For instance, have you heard the one about...

PROFESSOR: Yes.

GERALD: ...about the orang-utang who ate a pomegranate with a banana?

STEPHENSON: No?

GERALD: No, well, I don't really think it survives the translation, but it was very, very funny at the time.

STEPHENSON: I see. Well, Professor, to come back to my earlier question...how has Gerald reacted to being separated from his "family"?

PROFESSOR: Well, in the early days, Gerald made attempts to contact his own "flange" of gorillas...

GERALD: It's a "whoop", Professor, a "whoop" of gorillas. It's a "flange" of *baboons* for God's sake.

PROFESSOR: I mean, he used to write them the occasional letter. But it seemed a bit pointless after a while. They'd only eat them, or wipe their bottoms with them.

GERALD: Look, I know you've never got *on* with my mother...

PROFESSOR: Well she never exactly liked *me* either, did she?

GERALD: She got on fine with David Attenborough!

PROFESSOR: David Attenborough! David Attenborough! All I ever hear is David Bloody Attenborough!

GERALD: Look, let's leave Dave out of this shall we?

Gerald adores flower arranging. Here he puts the finishing touches to a display of giant lilies. (Gorilla, yes. Lilies, no. I don't believe a syllable of this article—Ed).

PROFESSOR: Oh, have a banana.

GERALD: All right I will.

STEPHENSON: Yes, well, Gerald, could I turn to you now.

GERALD: Yes, of course. Er...could you possibly pass the cream? Thank you. Yes, do go on.

STEPHENSON: Er...I believe you've been earning money doing TV commercials and so on. What do you spend your earnings on?

GERALD: Well, I suppose you expect me to say I spend it all on peanuts, bananas and carpet cleaner.

STEPHENSON: No, of course not.

GERALD: No, well, in fact I do spend about 95 per cent on those items, but the rest goes on little luxuries. I'm very keen on Johnny Mathis at the moment...

Gerald the gorilla enjoys a joke with Mrs Indira Ghandi and the Chief Marketing Director, Brylcreem Ltd. (No. No. And no. Drivel, all of it—Ed).

NOT! HE GOT OFF

PROFESSOR: And don't we know it? *When A Child Is Born* blaring out from our bedroom into the small hours when I'm trying to get some work done...

GERALD: Listen, the production on that album is amazing...

PROFESSOR: This is supposed to be my serious scientific project...

GERALD: *Your* scientific project? Listen, I went to evening classes for *three years!*

PROFESSOR: Oh shut up about your evening classes.

GERALD: I mean as Aristotle has it, 'η λυναιχα ειναι το ποδιγατψ; η ζψηθ ειται εν'ανγουφι''

PROFESSOR: You arrogant little bastard. This is my work you're wrecking. You think it's easy for me?

GERALD: Easy for you! I'm in quarantine half the year! Whenever we go somewhere I'm stuck in the chain locker.

PROFESSOR: Trampling the garden! Eating all the daffodils!

GERALD: I do *not* eat daffodils!*

Gerald is a successful novelist with a string of best sellers to his credit. (Hmm.—Ed).

STEPHENSON: Well, thank you both very much, perhaps we can leave it there. Professor, Gerald, thank you.

PROFESSOR: Thank you.

GERALD: Thank you.

*A MORI Opinion Poll conducted amongst a representative sample of the plants in Professor Fielding's back garden, and an interview with one of the leading daffodils will appear in next week's issue.

NEXT WEEK: ECOLOGY
How to convert your comfortable holiday cottage into a derelict barn.

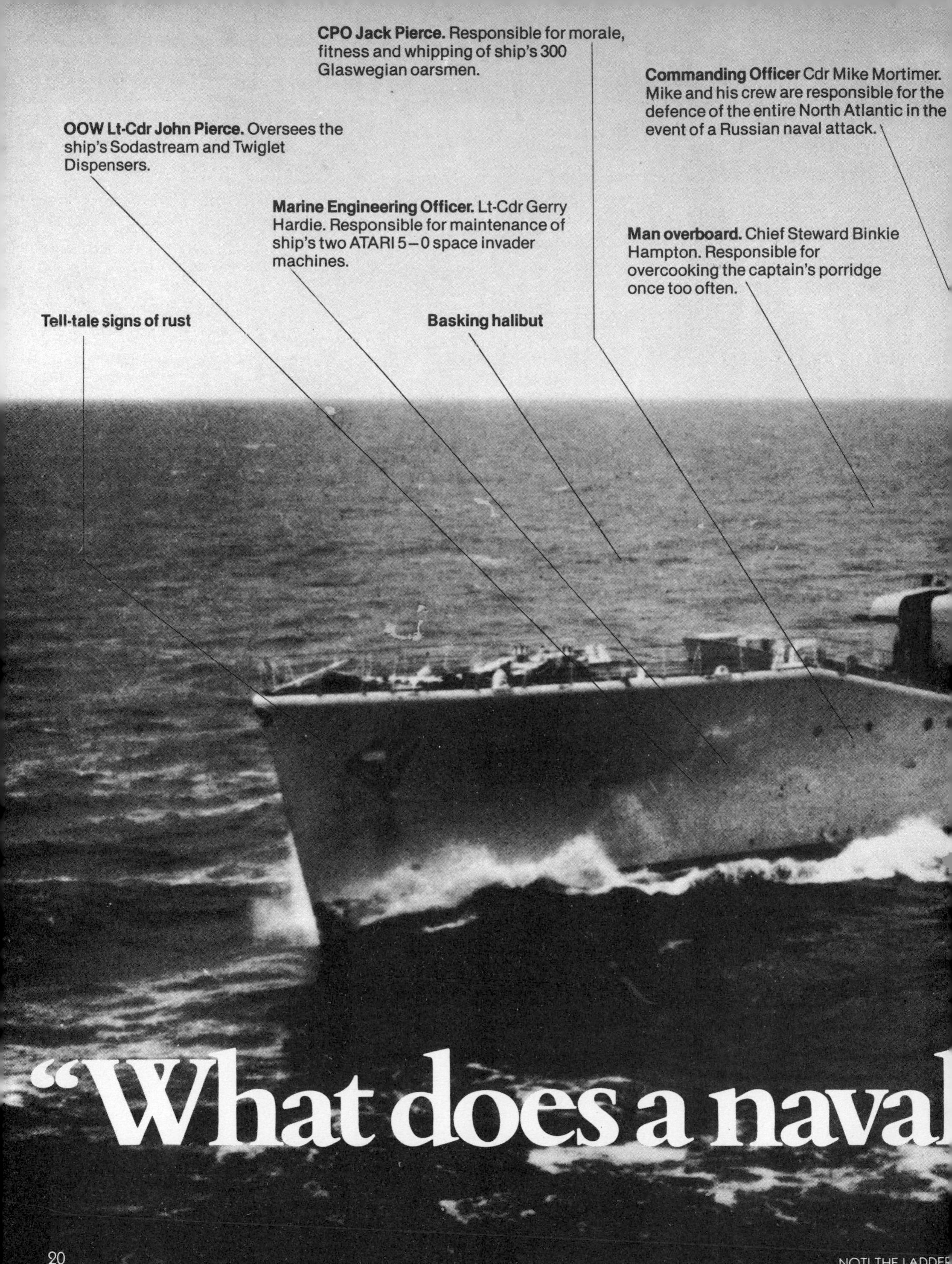

OOW Lt-Cdr John Pierce. Oversees the ship's Sodastream and Twiglet Dispensers.

CPO Jack Pierce. Responsible for morale, fitness and whipping of ship's 300 Glaswegian oarsmen.

Commanding Officer Cdr Mike Mortimer. Mike and his crew are responsible for the defence of the entire North Atlantic in the event of a Russian naval attack.

Marine Engineering Officer. Lt-Cdr Gerry Hardie. Responsible for maintenance of ship's two ATARI 5−0 space invader machines.

Man overboard. Chief Steward Binkie Hampton. Responsible for overcooking the captain's porridge once too often.

Tell-tale signs of rust

Basking halibut

"What does a naval

Rear Admiral Chief Bghani Sowante. On loan from Zimbabwe Naval Reserve under Commonwealth Officer Exchange scheme. His opposite number will spend two years beagling in and around the Wankie National Game Reserve.

Basil Thompson Esq., Radio Rentals repairman.

Observer single-handed transatlantic yachtsman. Bill Norris, Mate of captain.

Brigadier-General Sir Luke Urquhart. Finds water-skiing opportunities better in the Navy.

Lt Jeremy Parker. Impersonates Prince Andrew at foreign ports of call.

1st Battalion Red Army Marine Commando. Responsible for sabotage, spying, shipboard entertainment.

F65

officer do, exactly?"

NOT! AND ENTERED

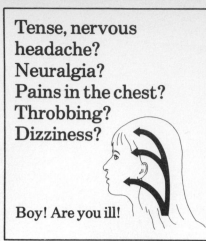

Tense, nervous
headache?
Neuralgia?
Pains in the chest?
Throbbing?
Dizziness?

Boy! Are you ill!

Sam is forty-one. He has no money, and he doesn't know where the next penny is coming from. But he knows where it is going to.

For Sam is a Newspaper Appeal Victim. Each year many thousands of people suffering from the psychological disorder of giving money away to charity become homeless, having donated everything they own.

Some of the worst cases are even driven to theft, robbing for large sums of money in order to raise what they consider to be a charitable donation, and satisfy their craving to give. They need help. Financial help. For they are tragic people. Penniless and walking the streets. They need money. And company. Now.

Help these people back into society again. We beg you, plead with you please, to send everything you can afford. Steal if you have to. But please send something, however large, to *The Newspaper Appeal Victims Appeal.* Anyone can help. No one is too poor to contribute. And that includes you Sam.

Newspaper Appeal Victims Appeal,
PO Box 47, Oxford.
Give now, get later.

Two new amazing popular magazines from *Recondite Press Ltd*

Out this month!!

Human waste is one of the world's richest sources of methane. Yet what do we do with it? We throw it away. Literally. This nation could be self-sufficient in crude within a year if we obey one simple rule. Save it. The British have always had it in them to cope in a crisis and British know-how leads the world in methane conversion technology.

And now you can share in this revolution with your own PO-PED.

The PO-PED is the product of a unique collaboration between the finest minds of both Honda and British Leyland. The frame, engineering and radio are Japanese. But all the porcelain and enamelware are British.

Yours to enjoy in the privacy of your own road.

PO-PED

STOUT LIFE
All The News That's Fat To Print

PROUD TO BE STOUT

Finding Our Feet

It's about this time of year when Christmas seems so far away, and Pancake Tuesday looks like its never going to come that stouts everywhere are thinking of tightening their belts. This must not happen! News has reached us of two hamburger joints closing in Streatham. A stout sister has written from Inverness of harassment at *The Bide A Wee Griddle* counter. Worst of all, a health shop has opened in Huddersfield. Stouts - 'Stand up and be counted'. The world wide conspiracy that has for so long threatened those of the flabby persuasion is strengthening its grip on the fabric of the straight society. There has never been a time when action has been more urgently needed. There has never been a time when the slim-orintated media have screamed and ranted so resolutely of excess and overeating. Every day new so-called slimming publications hit the street. It's invidious. It's degrading. It's arguably the greatest denial of human rights since the H-Block canteen was blown up. And yet. And this is a big *yet*, where are those brothers and sisters who were out in force in the heady days of the *Bring a bun and spaghetti rallies*? We ate together in those days, when the sun shone and the *Gayn Wate Fun Drink* flowed. We lay out on the grass and saw a bright future, a fat future when stouts and stoutesses would walk, nay run, nay wobble, down any street in this land dressed in bikini briefs and shout "Look!" "Look at me! This is my flab. This is my paunch! These are my outsize hips, size forty and above! Lay hold of my stoutness and be not afeared." And today? Sales of *Diet Pepsi* have never been higher. We know who's buying it. You know who's buying it! Eat now. Tomorrow may be too late.

The Appeal

September the tenth has now been set as the date for Regina vs. Stout News in court number 20, Old Bailey, Widnes. The fight goes on to prevent the so-called Viewers and Weight-Watchers Association and other right-wing skinny pressure groups invoking an obsolete obesity law against the News, following the publication of Binky Kirkup's poem *The Urge at Midnight*. Professor Kirkup is no longer in England. He is currently teaching at the University of Bilbao, Hong Kong. (Messages of support c/o The Gourmet Rendezvous and Massage Parlour, John le Carre Boulevard, Hong Kong East). Professor Kirkup has written a follow-up to the first sonnet, entitled *The Urge at Midnight II* which we publish in full.

Further donations are required to fight this case. Money should be sent to: 'The Urge at Midnight Fighting Fund', 25 Lymph Passage, London NE2

THE URGE AT MIDNIGHT FIGHTING FUND. WEEK FORTY-FIVE. Now stands at - £000000.000.000.24p (Some foreign coins and a Bell Fruit token)

Contributors so far:
Anon.
L Goodman (no relation)
Archy and all at the Rise__
Gresham Stouts
Dave Wing-Marky
Dinky Kirkup
The Soweto Sisters
The Rev Canaan Banana
The Salvation Army Peace
   Corps (Longford Branch)
The TUC
Russ Abbott
Dr Timothy Fielding
Francis (Fatboy) Raffles
Tiptree Agricultural
   Machinery Slush Fund
P Dempster
Q Dempster
Z Dempster
Mrs Dempster
Ronnie Reynalde
Rita and her Gazpachoes
   (No sole agent)
Fred Timms Q.C.
Dr Blood
Benny Green
Lester Piggott

Another fund raising gig will be held next week at the Lewisham Palais. The bill includes the Freddie Truman Allstars, Douglas Adams, Smartie and the Pants (featuring Willi Warma). Plus half of Rowan Atkinson.

THE URGE AT MIDNIGHT II

Roland Kirkup

Ease.
A troubled bag of chips,
That's all.
Falangetincise a gracious
           moment.
Oh God I wept.
Again.
Oh God I wept.
An empty Fridge.
Tomato Sauce.
Stale Bread.
And to cop
it all
the all night caff is
closed.
Dear oh dear.

Letters

Letters for publication should be addressed to:
Stout Life,
Elephantiasis House,
Bath Lane, Staines.

While your film critic was quite right to condemn CRUISING as a viscious film, surely he missed the point when he claimed the film was anti-stout. Admittedly one slightly overweight chap was pushed out of the way early on, but otherwise the whole film seemed to be about gays doing each other in. Surely it should be us gays who should be offended?
Griff Rhys-Jones,
The Tent, Hampstead Heath.

Yea O.K. But it's typical of the pouffs to get hot under the collar cos a few of them get chopped about a bit. But let's face it that's what happens to perverts. We're all sick to the back teeth with Gays waggling their horrible doings under our noses. Why don't you stand back Nancy Boys because the Stouts are coming through!
Marcus Pouncer

The Editor would like to make it clear that the views expressed in this paper are not necessarily those of the management.

That's because you're one of them anyway!
Marcus Pouncer

Come Off It

In a recent issue of your publication a photograph of our Client - Mr Cliff Michelmore, the esteemed broadcaster and travel expert was published, alongside the direct assertion that the said Mr Michelmore was 'Stout'. Since Mr Michelmore is not in the slightest bit stout this has caused him and his family the gravest personal offence. We will expect an apology printed in full or further steps will be taken.

Here's another piccie of Big Boy Cliff from our 'Burst Out Of The Closet' file.

World Summit Meets

World leaders from all the major Western countries met here today in the *Palais de Maurice Chevalier* for extended discussions on matters of international importance. The meeting, expected to last at least five days has been called in the face of increasing East/West tension over the last few months. Due to address the assembled Premiers tomorrow, the Commander in Chief of Nato Forces flew in yesterday and is expected to give a press conference later this afternoon. (Tea time). Despite the amount of time available extensive investigations have revealed that the summit will not be devoting any of the conference to Stouts and their problems. This will come as a bitter blow to Stouts everywhere, particularly in the light of yesterdays revelations that the twenty three previous summits have not discussed Stouts either. A spokesman I questioned earlier today (Breakfast time) was adamant that the conference would not touch on Stouts.

So there you have it. Nothing. Niet. Rien. Nowt! Nothing whatsoever on Stouts. I tried to find out what they were going to eat at the banquet tonight but they wouldn't tell me. So there it is in black and white, here in this freezing cold hell-hole up in the Alps, miles from a good restaurant, for the fifth time this year and still not a word about Stouts. Not a murmur. Stumm. O.K.?

ARTIFAT
Stout Gruntshop

Pigs Can Fly

Currently the only theatre group in the country that is attacking the establishment in its hard middle, GRUNTSHOP's latest offering is a savage indictment of the elitist, exploitative basis of so-called existential theatre. It effectively demonstrates how Stouts have been stereotyped by a fascist media into ignoring the complex issues that face them today. On the surface three people eat twenty seven sandwiches in the space of half an hour. Underneath, the observant spectator, (and that is not a word that Gruntshop would like because they are basically into audience participation in a big way. One of the audience ate a whole roast ox during the proceedings) can percieve a complex Weltanschauung. The set made of millions of rubber sausages is just one example. Five quid may seem a lot to pay for half an hour of theatre, but Gruntshop include their usual fried Mashed Potato with Spaghetti Balls in the price and five intervals to eat the second helpings.

　　　　　　　　　-TUBBS

The Old Vic Company

Othello

After all the ballhoo in the press earlier in the week as the establishment critics rushed to defend their precious bard from the manglings of a well-known film star, it is hardly necessary to point out that Joan Collins was never destined for the title role anyway. Inevitably, however, they all missed the central point: when is the OLD VIC going to widen its seats? The play, some sort of sixteenth century exercise in racism is at least an hour too long, but it seemed like even longer to your reviewer who was stuck in a stall three sizes too small for him. There is only one interval. Ice-creams were not on sale.　　　R.B.

DISH OF THE DAY!
Keeping in shape: Fatmate Mel warms up with a tempting blend of doughnuts & maple syrup. Henri Fudge for the Pie Centre, Lewisham.

Movies In Brief

APOCOLYPSE NOW
W.E. and other venues.

And not a moment too soon if you ask me. A load of emaciated skins buggering around in a boat during a war somewhere. You'd be much better off in an eaterie.

LA BOUEFF BOURGINOGNE DE MONSIEUR HENRI
Screen on the Carpark.

Classic. Featuring Lorraine (la Grosse) Quiche, this is a typical sparse masterpiece from Truffle. So sparse in

fact that you'll be able to get round to Mario and Dando's Trattoria Bustigutta in good time.

PSYCHO
Cinecenta, Lesta Squair.

The skinny did it.

PEOPLE BEING CHOPPED TO PIECES WITH MACHINE TOOLS, HACK SAWS, PEN-KNIVES etc
Essoldo Arts Complex.

Posing as a cheap exploitation flick this is in fact a film about people being chopped to bits with machine tools, hack-saws, pen-knives etc. A deeply moving film, but liable to put you off your hamburgers.

JAWS
Scene 98, Swiss Centre.

Not what it might seem unfortunately. Some rubbish about a fish (inedible).

THE EMPIRE GETS A KICK UP ITS ARSE
London Film Makers Co-op and House Moving Service.

Part fifteen of the Darth Vader Saga. Within the format of superior sci-fi Lucas continues to unfold much deeper themes of Angst and Reichian parapsychology: witness the flying weetabix at the end of reel one. A must.

ARTIFAT
Lonely Paunches

ARE YOU VERY ATTRACTIVE, interested in things physical, sensitive non-smoker and enormously fat who wishes to meet similar? I'm not, but there you go. BOX 11007

STOUT interested darts, dart-boards, pointed things with feathers (or plastic), round things made of wood, late night BBC 2 Television, Leighton Rees etc. wishes to meet similar, view partnership. (Must like cricket).　　BOX 99013

SLIM LOOKING attractive chap who at age thirty has just accepted fact he's stout wishes to find

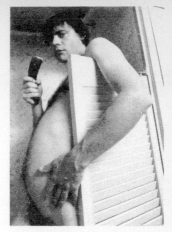

'Squeeze Out Of The Closet!'

intelligent, clean-shaven, non scene, attractive, fast-talking, straight-looking, smooth-operating, clean-living, masculine-behaving Pepsi Cola machine, with a view lasting relationship. BOX 2843

BLACK GUY seeks green.
　　　　　BOX 443112

ARIES STOUT GUY seeks forward looking Piscean Female to bore silly with astrology, horoscopes, occult and other mindless nonsense.　　BOX 99117

HELP! I am a normal (!!) attractive (?) affection-ate(@) kinda guy (%) but my typewriter seems to have brok/2. BOX *!!½%

NON-STOUT 5'4", 22 stone seeks similar to burst out with.　　　BOX 853192

PURPLE GUY, seeks orange-spotted.　　BOX 66431

WANTED ZANY STOUT into repeating Monty Python Sketches complete with funny accents and rolling eyes to beat over head with heavy club.
　　　　　BOX 15129

PROFESSIONAL STOUT GUY, available guy fawkes parties etc. BOX 82281

SHY BUT FORTHCOMING, tall, short, stout, skinny seeks similar for uncomplicated relationship.　BOX 64444

VERMILLION STRIPED GUY seeks patchy blue.
　　　　　BOX 91718

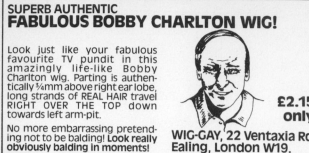

NOT! GRASPED HER

'Amis Boy', the horse that came last in the 3.30 at Cheltenham on Saturday.

First Day of the Vegetarian Game Shooting Season.

The Kuwaiti Swimming Team training for the 1984 Olympics despite conditions of severe drought.

LUCAN TO SIGN FOR SECOND SEASON AT BRISTOL CITY

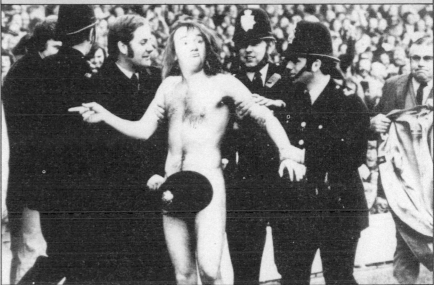

Police arrest Lord Lucan at the Bristol City ground on Saturday, his appearance hideously disfigured by plastic surgery.

Lord Lucan, the missing Earl hunted by police for two years, has been found. He has been playing centre forward for Bristol City FC for the whole of last season. Arrested last Saturday in a lonely spot unfrequented by the general public, the last twenty minutes of the second half were played without him. The Earl was quoted as saying: 'It's a fair cop, officer. I'm relieved it's all over, that is all. I had hoped to remain in obscurity, but now I am looking forward to rejoining normal society as a useful member of the human race'.

The Manager of Bristol City FC, who refused to be named, said today: 'I'm delighted personally. I never believed he was dead. Now I am confident that many of the rest of the team will be found alive. Or arrested. I don't care.' He confirmed that the Earl will definitely be remaining with the club. 'I don't know why,' he said, 'maybe I'm just an old softie, maybe it's because very few own goals have ever been scored from the Maximum Security Wing of the Scrubs'.

DAILY STAR Spot The Ball Competition

Last Week's Winner Ball correctly spotted by Mr E. Heffer, London

PICTURE: PLACE 'X' HERE

APPLICATION FORM
Daily Star Spot The Ball Competition.
The contest is open only to the editors and employees of the Daily Star, their readers and friends and anyone else who finds anything more intellectually taxing than gawping at pictures of young women with their clothes off a bit of a pain in the old behind.
HINT: The ball is the big round thing right in the middle of the picture that all the players are looking at.

NAME: PLACE 'X' HERE

Declaration: I am over 18, but don't wish to behave as if I am.

MEN!

Do you hunger for Arianna Stassinopoulos?

Do you yearn for beautiful, exciting, enormous Arianna?

Do you wish Arianna could be yours every night, just the way she is on television every night?

Well, now you can have her! Yes, you can have your own incomprehensible Greek sex symbol with —

THE INFLATABLE ARIANNA STASSINOPOULOS DOLL!

*Your inflatable Arianna Doll is not only life-like, she's life size!
*She's easy to inflate, with her own built-in inflator.
*And equally easy to deflate!
*She has TWO outstanding points.
*And THREE orifices — and *all* of them talk continuously!

WARNING: DO NOT OVER-INFLATE

The Arianna Doll comes direct to you by mail. You can return her unused within 14 days, if not completely exhausted.

☐ *NO thank you, definitely not.*
☐ *NO, no, please I implore you.*
   Tick your choice.

We care.

We care about people. Deeply. Vaguely. Many parts of the world are not very nice. We want to help. Help us find out which parts they are. Or whatever. You know.

? AMNESIA INTERNATIONAL

PO Box either 207, or 702, or 027,
That Big Town With The Exhibition Centre And all The Tunnels, Can't Remember The New Name Of The County But It Used To Be Called Rutland Or Something. Anyway, You Can't Miss It. BM9 3TX.

LEFT: The U.S. Nude Cross-country Scrabble Team in action. (They were later disqualified after the Judges Ruling the LUILNSOIN is not a proper word.)

BELOW: Procelebrity Skateboarding Three contestants in trouble at Wednesday's Heats in Cardiff.

Forgot to let go!

Forgot to bend knees!

Forgot to bring skateboard!

This week's Spot The Gob Competition

Last month's QPR v Celtic Game. A great match with some masterly dribbling by all.

Place greasy mark on picture where you think the gob is. Answers in a stamped addressed plastic bag to:
'Spot the Gob', Not! Magazine, London W1

Accept any of these lovely volumes **Absolutely Free** *

(Books shown, left to right:)
101 THINGS THAT CAN GO WRONG WITH A DC 10 — BOEING PUBLICATIONS — *Counts As One Choice*

Elizabeth David's BAD BREATH COOKERY

THE LADYBIRD POP-UP BOOK OF ACNE — ERIC ZIT

The Diary of CAPTAIN OATES

IDI AMIN'S Cooking with People — *£3 Published Price*

Cambridge University Press ENGLISH-RIPPONESE RIPPONESE-ENGLISH Dictionary

£92 Club Price — *The Worry of Sex* — DR ALEX DISCOMFORT

The Devil Rides About A Bit — *Denis Wheatley*

IS HE FAKING IT TOO? XAVIERA HOLLANDER — *£79.62 Club Price*

My Father Couldn't Spell Ronald — 'The Confessions of Roald Dahl'

THE GOOD KIOSK GUIDE — THE CAMPAIGN FOR REAL STRING

The Observer's Book of RABIES SYMPTOMS — *£4.35 Published Price*

as your introduction to the **Irish Book Club** ☘

YES! We dare you to accept our incredible offer of these delightful tomes in luxurious kowloon, garnished with sateen bookmarks, sturdy flyleaves and brand-new antique engravings. We are so proud of the wondrous sheen of the glistening typefaces, the creamy sensual feel of the rich Swedish larch paper, and the delicious booklike shape of these articles that we are squirming with pleasure. Well!

AND YET! You may even want to *read* some of them! Thrill to the endless chapters of Harold Wilson ("I laughed till I was made a peer" — Daily Mirror. "A week is a long time in a preface" — Milton Shulman). Weep openly with Captain Oates' tale of what happened when he came back into the tent after going outside for a little while. Hear his terrible words "Day 16. Cannot go on much longer. Last night we ate the last of the stenographers. Can no longer type fast enough with mittens on. Must risk frostbite to meet deadline. Have thought of good exit line 'I'm just stepping out for some carbon paper. I may be some time'."

WHY JOIN? Hear what our Series Editor, Janet Street-Porter has to say: "Oi awarg uwushmulsh ar dunnao, owoprsh nurb warrl".

HUGE SAVINGS! Lots of very interesting titles in the picture! Many more books to come in the next six months, and none of them as good value as the ones pictured here!!

YES! You too can become a member of the Irish Book Club! With the Irish Book Club you receive all the books of your choice as often as you want, with no obligation, and **ABSOLUTELY FREE**, and we lose an awful lot of money.

> **The Black Arts: a message from Denis Wheatley**
>
> Do not under any circumstances tamper with the black arts because you're likely to make a lot of money and as you know money is the root of all evil and anyway there isn't room for two of us on this patch.

ACCEPT 250 VOLUMES FOR NOTHING IMMEDIATELY*

*If a reigning monarch of a Western European nation.

1980
A REAR VIEW

JANUARY: The New Welsh Volunteer Fire Brigade in action.
FEBRUARY: The Pope selects a new Catholic-approved coitus-interruptus position.
MARCH: London Transport's new vandal-proof one-man bus.

APRIL

AUGUST

APRIL: New developments in the hunt for ex-Emperor Bokassa.
MAY: Mr Bill Sirs after shop stewards presented him with a token of appreciation for his handling of the steel strike.
JUNE: The Mayor of Dublin lays the foundation stone for the first in a series of high-rise bomb shelters.

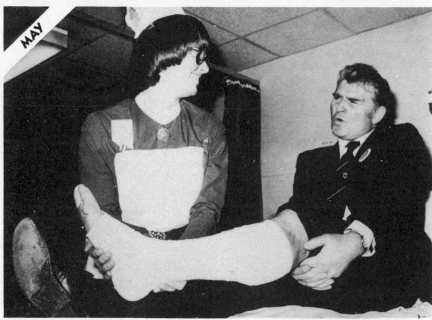

MAY

SEPTEMBER

JUNE

JULY

JULY: After the simulated NATO attack on the UK, Mrs Thatcher takes delivery of the remains of the RAF.
AUGUST: Desmond Wilcox retires to devote his life to supervising production of Esther Rantzen's dental floss.

NOT! THE OTHER SIX

SEPTEMBER: Prisoners at Parkhurst celebrating after Mrs Thatcher's announcement that long-term inmates will be encouraged to buy their own cells.

OCTOBER: Fears for President Carter's sanity increase after he is seen at a protest rally calling for his own resignation.

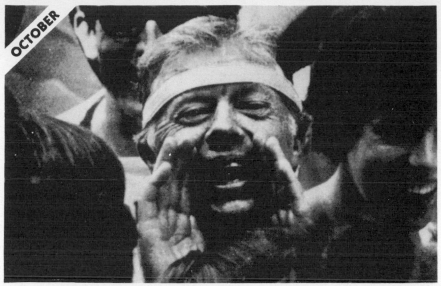

NOVEMBER: A group of British adulterers awaiting the traditional punishment of an Islamic Court in Riyadh.

DECEMBER: Mark Thatcher practising eagerly before opening the Christmas present from his mother: A Blow-Up Arianna Stassinopoulos Doll.

WHO'S WHO
SCREWING

with Mandy Mandrax

Have I just been run off mon pieds! Don't ask! I spend aujourdhui in a state of total and utter excretement!

Yesterjour began at London's Inn on the Park at a Fancy Dress Charity in aid of the Save the Alligator Handbag Campaign. We all had to come as our favourite hors d'ouevres...

Bill Gibb ran up a stuffed artichoke for me. But in the parking lot I bumped into **Pete Townsend** dressed as a large portion of taramosalata and **Rod Stewart** who'd come as a sardine vol au vent. There was a hideous mix-up in the lobby so the three of us went in together as ratatouille in a basket.

Shared a joke with **Jackie Onassis** who'd come as a portion of yesterday's whitebait. Then spotted **Britt Ekland**, who disgraced herself by climbing onto a trolley as a Caesar's salad and then tossed herself. **Victor Lownes** asked her to leave so she threw herself on the chandelier and hung by her anchovies.

Just then, in came **The Three Degrees** – stark naked, backwards, and pretending to be one and a half avocadoes.

But the hit of the party was my dearest friend **Gore Vidal.** He arrived without a costume and they simply wouldn't let him in. So he sneezed on himself and came in as an oyster! My dears, I laughed until the prawns ran down my cheeks!

Afterwards, I whirled off to Plumpies, London's most exclusive health club – so select they don't take fat people. There, as usual, I met my oldest friend, **Margaret Trudeau,** having her unsightlies pruned yet again. My dears, you could crochet that woman! Margaret tells me that **Liz Taylor** has had her face sewn back so often she's facing the other way. And **Omar Sharif?** Well, he has to go to a taxidermist twice a week just to stand up!

Then, bombe surprise, who should wobble in but my oldest friend, **Joan Collins.** We waited for a few minutes till her behind arrived. Then the three of us sat on it and talked yoghourt. Joan is so fascinating – once you get her on the subject of carbohydrates and lymph nodes. I remember Joan once saying to me that she gets a lot of fatty deposits around her ganglions. She's really marvellous!

Finally, girls, if you were repelled by the harpoon sequence in Moby Dick, you

Joshua Nkomo speaks of Robert Mugabe's 'deep love' for Lord Carrington, and shows how close they have got.

should have seen my old friend **Diana Dors** having acupuncture!

I then literally leapt out of the jacuzzi and off to Regine's for Disco. All were there. Everyone had to come as their alter ego. There were fifty-six Hitlers and twenty-nine Marilyn Monroes and all of the girls came as they were.

My oldest friend **Michael Caine** came as an ostrich because he couldn't read the invitation.

My oldest friend **Mick Jagger** came over to me and said in his usual satirical way that his halibut was overcooked! He makes me laugh so much!

Princess Caroline's laundress Eva spent the whole evening boasting that she had swallowed one of **Bjorn Borg**'s socks. Very boring but sweet.

Finally, here's my Tip of the Week... when it comes to those little nose jobs – remember the holes point downwards!

Hasta lasagne!

RIGHT: Mrs Shirley Williams in her office.

MOVEMENTS
Died, moved on etc.

Birthdays
Ex-President Idi Amin, 50 this week, is leading a life of luxury in Libya. Last week he bought a microwave oven that seats eight. And **Tony Blackburn** is 61 today. He has lost 2½ stones recently, but now his agent reports he's lost his catapult as well.

Illnesses
Man about town **Roddy Llewellyn** has sympathised with **Prince Charles** who has been suffering from heat exhaustion. Roddy says he gets the same thing if he sunbathes for more than ten months at a time. And **Prince Charles** has regretted the outcry

over his use of the word 'knackered' to describe his condition, and says next time he feels shagged out he'll keep his gob shut. **Ayatollah Khomeini**, 106, is reported to be having trouble with the Kurds again, but doctors say it's not uncommon at his age. He is fighting fit and will probably live for another fifteen years. His condition is described as unsatisfactory.

Returned

Singer **Englebert Humperdinck** has returned from Las Vegas, weighing three stone lighter. He's shaved off his sideburns.

Died

Another of **Robert Mugabe**'s former guerrilla commanders has been refused service in a Salisbury hotel for not wearing a tie. The manager was later sacked for not wearing a head.

En route

Pope John Paul II continues his hit tour of South America this week. Some observers speculate that he is experimenting with mass rallies as an alternative to birth control in containing the population explosion. At his last one twice as many people were killed as at the average **Who** concert.

Yasser Arafat at PLO Press Conference. Quote: "If Reagan wins the election I'll eat my red and white tea-towel".

DEATH OF BERNARD MANNING

We regret to announce that Mr **Bernard Manning**, the comedian who was told by his doctors to lose five stones or die, has today lost five stones.

Sayings of the week

■ Ian Smith was a venomous creature. In my dealings with him I found him to be an intriguer, a liar, a charlatan, a study in deceit. I liked him enormously.
Sir Harold Wilson on Rhodesia

■ I remember the days when you could go down to a cafe, have a slap up meal, get botulism, go to hospital, catch an infection, die, have a lovely, lovely funeral and still get change out of half a crown.
Barbara Cartland on the Twenties

■ I think I learned a great lesson from Chappaquiddick, a great lesson, and a lesson which many of my fellow Americans would do well to take cognisance of. And the lesson is this: 'Don't drive across narrow bridges when you're pissed out of your mind'.
Sen. Edward Kennedy on Chappaquiddick

■ In my country a man is always presumed innocent until found dead.
Col. Ghaddafi on Libyan Justice

What would you do if London flooded?

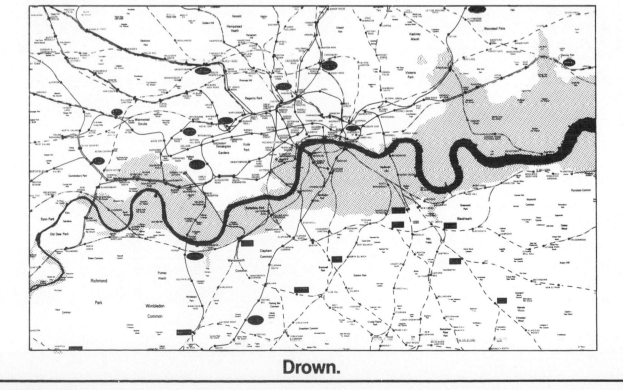

Drown.

Rev Tim Davis, Vicar.

NEW **Instant Pot Meals**
It's a bloody miracle!

Feeding five thousand hungry mouths wasn't easy for a working Messiah. Especially if he had as much housework as Tim here. How much easier it would have been if New Instant Pot Meals had been available then. Just add boiling water to one of these delicious fish-and-loaf flavoured snacks, and you have a tasty meal in seconds. With enough left over to fill twelve baskets!

As used by the Archbishop of Canterbury!

Bob Runcie writes:

My gargoyles just eap'em up

Queen for a week

Seven days in the life of a working monarch

Her Majesty and 'Blunty' go walkabout — delighting passers-by with their sense of fun.

Her Majesty travels incognito to Halifax and returns her Gannex.

Her Majesty attends the State Opening of Lord Goodman's new fridge.

Her Majesty has frank exchange of views with Iraqi Foreign minister on the question of reducing oil prices.

Her Majesty graciously continues to endure the stench of foreigners.

The man charged with snatching the Queen's handbag is released after Her Majesty fails to pick him out at an identity parade.

Her Majesty relaxes at home with friends.

DON'T LEAVE YOUR GOOLIES TO THE BALDIES.

MAKE A WILL.

That way there's less chance that if you snuff it in a car crash some vulture of a surgeon will come along and hack bits off you to stuff into some fat old coot who smokes too much.

Special offer to readers of this* magazine

Your chance to invest in the crafted beauty of tropical timber

A strictly limited edition of

Authentic Sandringham House-Party Corks

to commemorate HRH Prince Charles' 33rd consecutive winter holiday in Australia.

Lies alone cannot describe the exquisite elegance of these unique regal mementoes, each one a monument to the Royal Family's rare moments of relaxation. As you look at your collection of corks, you'll imagine in your mind's eye the precious liquid their removal unleashed, hear perhaps the soft rustle of headscarves, the distant whisper of a corgi breaking wind.   *or any other

Please send me a complete set of Authentic Sandringham House-Party Corks. This isn't the first time this has happened to me. I enclose a letter from my doctor explaining everything.

Name _____

Address _____

_____

THE ANCIENT JAPANESE ART OF
KALAMI

Things to do with Mel Smith

Kalami is the ancient Japanese art of folding road maps. First developed by Mogul hordes towards the end of the Ta'i dynasty, the practice reached the west in the mid-19th century when the 4th Earl of Sandwich found a slice of meat placed between two pieces of paper in his glove compartment.

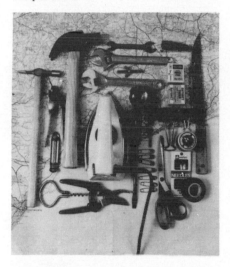

Competitive Kalami is now a popular feature of the annual Conference of Town Hall Planning Departments, and has recently been added to the curriculum at Sandhurst.

Here's a chance to try it yourself, using the Beginner's Kit (pictured above) and the Ordnance Survey First Series 1:50000 map of Eastbourne and Hastings (Sheet 199). Beginners should avoid the cloth edition.

1. First fold along the line of the A267 between Heathfield and Hailsham, taking care to by-pass Horam and Hellingly.
2. Score round the high-water line of Darwell Reservoir with the cap of a biro.
3. Make an incision along the length of the River Rother south of Stonegate.
4. Using a steam iron, trace the disused railway line that runs from Royal Tunbridge Wells to Hastings.
5. Place the second 'L' in Bexhill over the 'O' of Eastbourne and staple firmly.
6. Carefully insert the sheet between pages 211 and 212 of the AA 'Book of the Car'.
7. Place the book in the car boot *between* the spare tyre and the tool kit. Make sure the distilled water soaks into *all* the folds.

Hundreds of possibilities. A very nice hat . . .

. . . some lovely earrings . . .

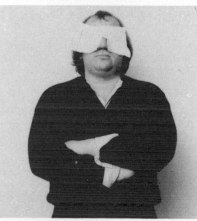

. . . a pair of sunglasses . . .

. . . a beautiful moustache . . .

. . . a charming bracelet . . .

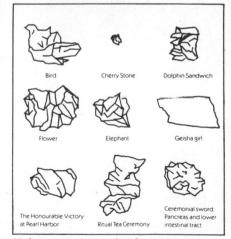

Bird   Cherry Stone   Dolphin Sandwich

Flower   Elephant   Geisha girl

The Honourable Victory at Pearl Harbor   Ritual Tea Ceremony   Ceremonial sword, Pancreas and lower intestinal tract

Make up your own, but here are some more ideas.

NEXT WEEK:
How to make your own Lesley Judd out of detergent bottles and alsatian's droppings.

NOSTRADAMUS YOUR STARS TOMORROW

Most astrologers will be telling you that with Venus in Mars at the moment, Saturn on the cusp of Mercury and the moon in the seventh house, now is traditionally an uneventful period in the lunar calendar. However, this month with Kadar in Buda, Sofia firmly ruled by Zvivkov, Leonid dominating the Kremlin and a Cretin in the White House, my own reading is very different. I predict that after lunch tomorrow a conventional tank attack by Warsaw Pact forces across the Czech border, followed by pre-emptive nuclear reprisals by the United States will result in the end of the world at about 3.27 pm. **The Weekend:** Rather quiet.

 SAUNA
(Dec 8–Jan 2)

A very long journey is advised as soon as possible.

Saunas are typically unambitious, so it's unlikely that you are a member of the Cabinet or a high-ranking Army Officer. Your lack of planning ability makes it improbable that you have obtained Swiss nationality, become an MP or ingratiated yourself with a bunker-owner. Still, you should have thought of that before, shouldn't you?

 GERULAITAS
(Jan 3–Jan 16)

Gerulaitases are organised and resilient folk. So no doubt you will already have whitewashed your windows, stuffed cardboard in the VentAxia etc. But don't worry about the expense now, you mean-minded little toad.

 NIMMO
(Jan 17–Jan 18)

You are due for surprise this afternoon. An old friend will drop in through the skylight in the kitchen and stain the sideboard. Try not to let your natural hospitality get the better of you. Stay under the table. Do not under any circumstance attempt to greet, tidy away etc your friend.

 HERPES
(Jan 19–Feb 28)

Your intelligence and sedentary disposition will be well suited to the latter part of the day. There's not going to be a lot going on after tea. You'll probably want to spend the time after lunch curled up with a book. But a word of warning: don't attempt any long novels at this time.

 MINIBUS
(Feb 29–May 23)

You are an ambitious person, as all Minibuses are, but your career will suffer a setback this afternoon. Get into work really early this morning and see if you can't get promoted a Grade or two by elevenses. Think again about refusing that posting to New Zealand last week, it's too late to do anything about it now, but you may like to consider whether being a social-climbing little megalomaniac has been worth it in the end.

 PERMUTIT
(May 24–June 4)
Early closing Weds.)

Your enquiring mind and passion for analysing the Meaning of Life calls for very fast thinking today. It may be best to spend the available time checking out off-the-peg religion.

 PILCHARD
(June 5–Oct 12)

As a Pilchard you are probably three inches long and encased in a tin of olive oil or tomato sauce. There is no need to be concerned about your position in society any more: indeed it may turn out to be a positive advantage.

 QUANGO
(Oct 13 only)

Quangos are great achievers – poets, scientists, sailors, commanders of Red Army Motorised Divisions etc. If the latter today should see positive action. If not, remember that Keats, Charlotte Bronte, and Alexander the Great were all quangos who died young.

 SERIES
(Oct 14–Nov 1)

All Series are men. So with old Harry Holocaust popping round for his Horlicks this afternoon, my advice to you is: sleep around a lot more. Now. There's no point in waiting for the four-minute warning and then relying on there being a natty bit of skirt on the next sandbag. If you've got wild oats as yet unsown, for God's sake sow the bloody things pronto because, in the words of our Lord, you can't take them with you when you go.

 MOULINEX
(Nov 2–Nov 28)

A predominantly female sign. My advice to you girls is the same; come on, lets start dropping them before they start dropping them. With luck, you may even feel the earth move.

 URINAL
(Nov 29–Dec 7)

Urinal's are great people (yes, I'm one). We also have extraordinary powers of prediction, and have already got the hell out. Bye bye.

 BIRO
(Today 12.30–
Tomorrow 4.00 pm)
Happy birthday.

FRED BASSET

Ho Hum! Looks like I'm in trouble.

THAT SODDING DOG HAS SHAT ON THE BED AGAIN

'The Confidence Trick'

Even for international statesmen, dental hygiene can be a real problem. Come the big day, other world leaders keep their distance. In today's world, halitosis and trench-mouth can mean the difference between peace and war. It took a Nobel prizewinner to crack the problem. And now, with DR. MENACHEM BEGIN'S KOSHER GUM SALVE you can feel confident. When it matters. Time after time. Let Dr. Begin put your money where your mouth is.

Works for armpits too!

Dr. Menachem Begin's Kosher Gum Salve

Dr. Begin's
Kosher
Gum
Salve

The Balance of Power in Europe

NATO

- Y Public relations officers
- Squash courts
- Swimming pools
- Towels
- Evening classes
- Parachute display teams
- White flags
- Allied jellyfish
- Regular rubbish collections
- Dirty weekends
- Ski slopes
- Yachting

Warsaw Pact

- Tanks
- Infantry divisions
- Inter-continental ballistic missiles
- Combat aircraft
- Bombers
- Warships
- Nuclear submarines
- Artillery divisions
- Helicopters
- Spies
- Satellites
- Olympic strongwomen

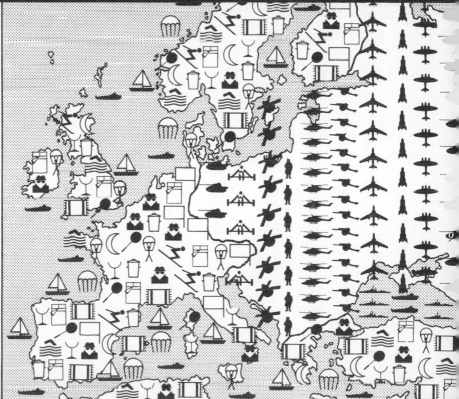

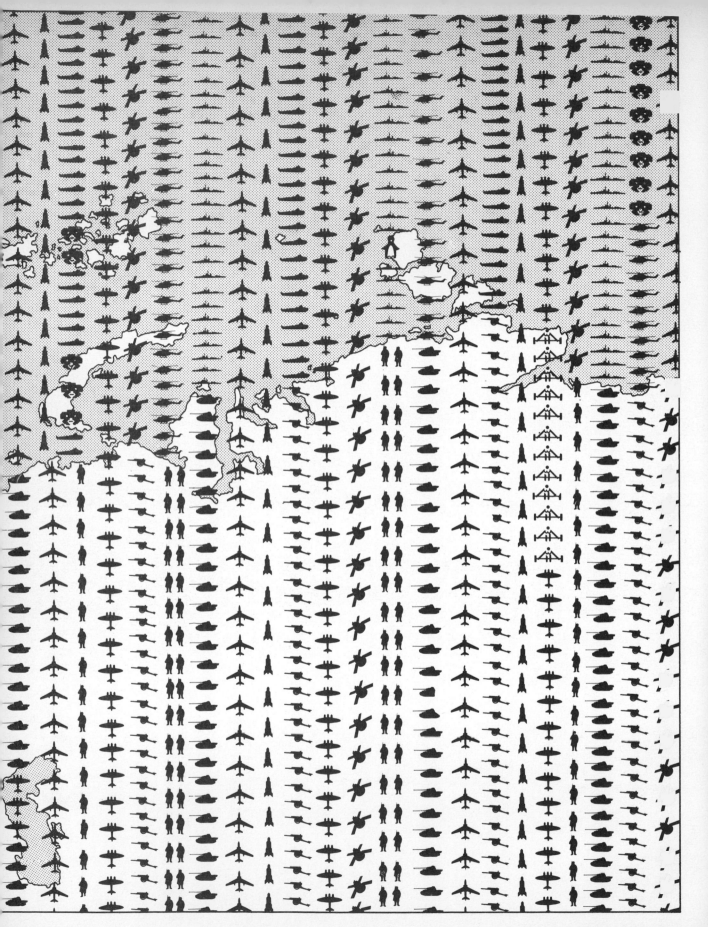

GUIDE TO THE WEEK

****
The number of stars indicates the quantity of drink taken during the Press Preview.

MONDAY
I'll Get It Darling! *****
9.30 pm Thames
New situation comedy from the writing team of Bob Deasey and Maurice Fote *(Not Today Thank You!, Don't Get Your Vicars In A Twist!* etc). Trouble in store for the sofa when Ros has to explain away a misunderstanding with the gasman — with hilarious consequences!

Panorama *
8.00 pm BBC1
David Dimbleby and Tom Mangold on Origami.

TUESDAY
Gala Concert **
10.30 pm Channel
Philharmonic conducted by Canaan Banana, with a programme that includes Haydn: *No 95* (The Excruciatingly Dull) *Symphony,* Laundromat's *Avocado Ma Non Troppo* and Nimmo's *Quartet for Strings and Relish Tray.*

Last Of The Summer Repeats
8.00 pm BBC1
Fred Heckmondwike tries Arthur's recipe for Lardy Cake.

Brucie's Back with Anthea Redfern (Friday, ITV)

Harry Worth (Monday, ITV)

WEDNESDAY
Play For Today **
9.30 pm BBC1
Gulp, by Gavin Toad. Set in a small Welsh weaving shed, *Gulp* looks at the events leading up to the abdication of Edward VIII through the eyes of a professional footballer and a politician's widow. Expensively directed by a member of the Socialist Workers Party.

Mae'n Naw O'r Gloch! ******
9.00 am BBC2
(Viewers in Wales get the programmes they deserve.)

THURSDAY
Spot The Cliché ***
7.30 pm Granada
New panel game, in which leading trade unionists have to speak for one minute without using the words "... referred to the National Executive".

On The Moov *
4.45 pm BBC2
Aids to literacy.

FRIDAY
Huge Fat Drunks Playing Darts ********
11.00 pm BBC2
What should be a really Titanic struggle between Dai 'Fatbelly' Gutbucket and the English champion, Tommy 'Even-fatterbelly' Belcher. Last week Belcher started strongly with

Mike Yarwood Impersonates Dave Allen (Wednesday, BBC 1)

THE GOODIES GO TO ITV where union rules have insisted that twelve Goodies are necessary instead of three (Thursday, LWT)

a triple brandy, a double vodka and four straight Bacardis, then missed a brown ale and finally lost his concentration altogether when a second pint scored and then came out again. Watch out for Gutbucket's technique with ice and lemon.

SATURDAY
Blake's Seven *
6.30 pm BBC1
Episode five: *The Death Lasers of Kraarn.* Gigantic Squids threaten to destroy the Universe, but the Doctor (Jonathan Miller) is trapped in the same concrete corridor as last week. Regulars

Late Night Horror — "The Thing That Crawled Out Of The Woolsack" (Saturday, BBC 2)

Zagglimorgz and the Talking Suitcase are joined by a miniskirted alien, an extra wearing a hat with rubber tentacles on, and guest stars Sirius and Thorax.

Badminton Horse Trials ********
10.30 pm BBC2
A chance to see the usual gang of horsey snobs riding into trees, falling into mucky ditches and making fools of themselves in public. Possibly without Princess Anne, who may have injured herself quite seriously at Burleigh last week judging by the way the crowd was laughing.

NOT! HER MOIST PUM

YOUR BODY

A completely unqualified hack journalist exposes details of your sick little mind to a huge readership.

When I was about 15, my father told me that playing with myself would stunt my growth, my friends told me that it would make me go blind, and teachers at school told me that it would rot my brain.

However, I ignored their advice completely. Now that everyone says 'Go ahead, play with yourself, it's normal, it's natural, it releases sexual tension and it's good for you', can you give me another excuse for why I am a 4'11" extremely short-sighted moron?

No.

I recently tried the new 'contraceptive sponge' which was recommended by my doctor, but I have discontinued it as I now have a cake in the oven. Is this right?

Yes.

Plans to donate Mark Phillips body to science had to be shelved this week after it was discovered that he still uses it on Saturday nights.

I would like some advice about how to obtain a 'termination'. I am a working mother with one child (a teenage son) and am not sure of the correct procedure. What would you advise?

How many months is it since conception?

Oh, I'm not sure. How old were you last birthday, Trevor?

Sixteen Mum.

It'd be about 192 months now, doctor.

Please go away and stop wasting my time.

Sticky times for the National Health Service.

John Corrie MP, introduces a new bill to clamp down on back-street acupuncturists.

My mother is the wrong side of 80, being now in her 64th year, and I am convinced that euthanasia is the answer. We were very impressed with the dignified way you bumped off old Mr Hoskins at No 32, and would like to know what choices are open to us. Can you help?

There are a number of methods and organisations which exist to deal with your problem, but I am willing to arrange the sad event myself for a very reasonable fee. In the domestic range I can offer 'Choking On A Fish Bone', 'Helping Her Under A Bus', and our 'Pot-holing Holiday In Cheshire' – which saves considerably on funeral costs. Drowning, however, is probably the simplest and most straightforward method.

That sounds nice and clean. How soon can you get here?

Thursday. But first you must decide what in.

I beg your pardon?

Please decide what you would like to have her drowned in. Sea, pond, fountain, municipal baths, under a tap, or the Olde English method – 'Drowning In A Butt Of Malmsey'.

Isn't that rather pricey?

Not at all. I understand that these days Sainsbury's do a very reasonable carafe.

She is very fond of soup – could she be drowned in soup, at all?

I think perhaps we ought to continue this conversation somewhere a little more discreet. I'll see you on Thursday afternoon.

My son was recently involved in a car accident, and parts of him used in a transplant operation. The doctor in charge told me there was nothing I could do as my son died of brain damage. What does this mean?

It means that the doctor cut out your son's brain and gave it to someone else.

Chinese scientists working on new cell-grafting techniques believe that it may now be possible to clone from a single Chinese person thousands of others – all completely different.

For the last few weeks I have been completely unable to feel my legs. What is the most likely explanation?

You've had your arms amputated.

A team of Nobel prize-winning dentists believe they may be close to solving the problem of Arthur Scargill's mouth.

LIFE OF PYTHON

One of the most controversial, and some would say, scurrilous films of the last year has been the box-office blockbuster, The General Synod's *Life of Christ*. <u>Sarah Gould</u> talked to Lawrence Vironconium – Bishop of Wroxeter, the director of the film, and Alexander Walker, one of its stoutest critics.

The film deals with the story of the rise of a humble carpenter's son, one Jesus Christ, to fame and greatness, but many people have seen in the film a thinly disguised and blasphemous attack on the life of Monty Python. Python worshippers say that it sets out to ridicule by parody the actual members of Monty Python who even to-day, of course, are worshipped and revered throughout the Western World.

NOT!: Alexander Walker, can I ask you first, what did you think of the film?

WALKER: It appalled me. I find it deeply offensive that, in what is still, after all, basically a Python-worshipping country, fourteen-year-old children can get to see this film. They get little enough proper Python these days, without having this distorted garbage paraded about.

NOT!: Bishop, you directed the film. Did you expect this kind of reaction?

BISHOP: Well, I certainly didn't expect the Spanish Inquisition! Yes. Yes, I did direct the film. And what I feel I *must* emphasise at once, is that it is not an attack on Python. I'm not a Pythonist myself, but obviously I have enormous respect for people, like Alexander, who are.

WALKER: Oh, come now bishop. The central figure in the film...this...er...

BISHOP: Jesus Christ.

Judas betrays Christ with a kiss.

ABOVE: "Suffer little children to come unto me . . ."
RIGHT: And they brought unto Him a woman taken in adultery . . .

WALKER: . . . thank you, this "Jesus Christ" is quite clearly a lampoon of the comic messiah himself, Our Lord John Cleese. I mean, look, even the initials are the same!

BISHOP: No. No, absolutely not. If I may try and explain. The Christ figure is not meant to *be* Cleese, he's just an ordinary person who happens to have been born in Weston-super-Mare at the same *time* as Mr Cleese.

WALKER: No. No, really, Lawrence, that's too . . .

BISHOP: And . . . and, if I may finish . . . he is *mistaken* for the comic messiah by credulous people of the sort that can see something "completely different" in anything, and who then follow him around in vast crowds . . . ah . . . doing silly walks, and chanting No, No, Not The Comfy Chair, and other slogans from the Good Bok itself.

NOT!: Alexander Walker – your comments on that?

WALKER: No, I'm sorry, whatever the Bishop may say, this is a highly distasteful film. Have people forgotten how Monty Python suffered for us? How often the

sketches failed? I mean these men died for us. Frequently.

NOT!: Bishop, turning back to you, do you not agree that the film may affect the position of Monty Python in our spiritual life?

BISHOP: No, I hardly think so. If Python *is* immortal (as Pythonists believe), I'm sure a mere film . . .

WALKER: A tenth rate film.

BISHOP: . . . I'm sure a mere film is not going to stop believers. Remember the

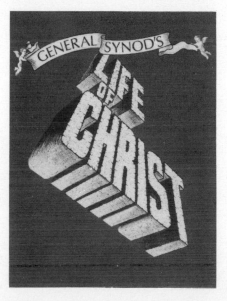

words of John Cleese: "When two or three are gathered together in my name, they shall perform the Parrot Sketch . . ."

NOT!: Indeed. "It is an Ex-Parrot . . ."

ALL: ". . . it has Ceased To Be".

NOT!: Well, the final scene in the film has perhaps attracted the most attention of all. Alexander Walker, a last word from you.

WALKER: Yes, well, the final scene is . . . is the ultimate blasphemy. It . . . it is set in a hotel, in Torquay, where literally hundreds of Spanish waiters are being clipped about the ear by this "Jesus Christ" bloke in a ghastly cartoon of the Comic Messiah's Greatest Half-Hour.

NOT!: Alexander Walker, thank you.

WALKER: Thank you.

NOT!: Bishop, thank you.

BISHOP: Thank you. Actually, it's not Torquay, it's Torbay.

WALKER: Oh, Torquay, Torbay, whatever. I really don't see . . .

NOT!: Alexander Walker, Bishop, thank you.

BOTH: Thank you.

NEXT WEEK: THE ISLAMIC NEW WAVE
Not! goes on location with '47 Brides for 7 Brothers

THE EVIL FLESH EATING FIENDS THAT ARE CORRUPTING BRITAIN

At 3.47 am on the morning of October 3rd 1980, a single chicken walked out through the gates of a low concrete building situated just off the A34 two miles south of Chipping Norton.

It made its way down the road, paused briefly to watch the grey blanket of a cold Cotswolds dawn lift softly off the distant beech groves of Wychwood Forest, then walked slowly back through the gates again. The time: 4.02 am (*See Map*).

Serve piping hot

The repercussions of that fateful saunter are still raging, for inside that building, we now know, animals are being specially bred. Not for scientific experiments, but for something far worse: *to be eaten by human beings*. Last year, in Britain alone, literally billions of innocent animals and birds simply disappeared. (*See Table*).

The Ones Who Never Came Back		
Figures supplied by Wilkinson Sword		
Cattle: 2,387 million		
Poultry: 764,000 million		
Sheep (Including Fish): 543 million		
Non-Vegetable Fats: 19%		
Emulsifier: 3.8%		
Monosodium Glutamate: .09%		

Laura Crawley is a veteran anti-vivisection campaigner, who runs an animal sanctuary at 'Sunnymead', near Tring.

"We get a lot of escapees here", she confirms, "sides of beef, country-style sausages, boil-in-the-bag venison – all kinds. Some of them reach us in a shocking condition, many haven't been fed for weeks."

Sizzling giblet gravy

For the unprepared, a visit to 'Sunnymead' can be a disturbing experience. And for Ms Crawley, 32, it has become a moral question.

The last stroll of chicken TF 544873.

'It's not just the suffering, the cruelty and the sheer brutality of it that upsets me. What makes me really angry is the way Maurice changed after the operation. I mean, he came to visit me in hospital, OK. But look at it from my point of view, right? Can you see any reason why three women who love each other can't provide a valid and nourishing home for any child, right? Or why three children can't create a significant living-space for me? Face it, Trevor, I'm a lonely person.'

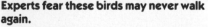

Experts fear these birds may never walk again.

Emergency Relief Supplies await shipment to Laura's Active Service Supermarket teams.

Ms Crawley's assistant Leo tends to the broken wings of a family bucket of Kentucky Fried Chicken.

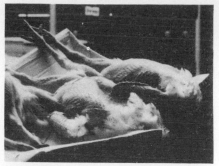

Help came too late for these Poussins Provençale

The animal-processing industry is, not surprisingly, reticent on the subject. We wanted to interview the notorious Max Von Turpitz, a 43-year-old Maltese-born carnivore who operates behind a cover-organisation called 'The Yorkshire Farmers

Toasted sheep's hearts

Society'. For weeks we were met by a stony silence, and it was only after we took the step of actually telephoning him in his office and making an appointment that he agreed to speak to us. In spite of all the evidence, he refused to admit to Laura Crawley's charge that he was degrading animals.

"Degrading them? Well, I don't think Miss Crawley's quite got the picture. We are murdering them, yes."

He was then asked whether he thought that the slaughter of his animals was a revolting and inhuman practice, but he brushed aside the question with a curt 'yes'. We suggested to Von Turpitz that he was the sort of blood-stained troll who would cheerfully gnaw the flukes off a sperm whale, but he would only say: "Sperm whale? Yes, I suppose I am. I like raw fish".

But this magazine is not satisfied by such glib disclaimers. And neither is Laura Crawley. She and her lobby are taking their case to the Human Rights Commission in Strasbourg, and are also planning to write to the Guardian Woman's Page. That done, Ms Crawley has set her sights on fresh targets: the psychiatric mistreatment of root vegetables.

The Intensive Care Unit.

NEXT WEEK:
Not! Probe continues the story with a Special Report: 'The Arable Farmers Who Starve Their Barley Of Conversation'.

The Blue Overall Triangle

Terrifying new evidence is emerging that in recent months more than 311 plumbers, summoned to jobs in London, have (though reported as having set off for their destination) mysteriously failed to arrive. Scientists believe that we may be under the influence of a malign area known as the Blue Overall Triangle, which covers approximately the whole of Britain, and inside which plumbers and other artisans simply disappear without trace.

Stone-age man believed that one day gasmen would come to mend his pilot light.

Public concern has been alerted largely through the reports of a Dr. Conrad Maelström of Stockholm University. He believes it is possible that such people

Ancient tomb carvings...or a garage estimate?

may be being kidnapped by aliens. He quotes the story of an electrician who claims to have experienced a 'close encounter' on a housing estate in Potters Bar last year.

The electrician, whose name is given only as Fred, reported: "It was...horrible. These sort of 'things' grabbed me and the next thing I knew they'd got me in this 'room', and forced me to, well...you know... *work,* on what I can only describe as 'a plug'." Fred, reports Maelström, was so traumatised by the experience that he cannot even bring himself to mend the lights in his living room.

Maelström cites the legend of Montezuma as evidence that this horrifying phenomenon is by no means new. The Aztecs, he says, waited 1000 years for the prophesied arrival of an AA repair man, and kept themselves amused building a civilization in the meantime. How could they, he asks,

have possibly known of the existence of AA men, who even now remain a theoretical concept?

Despite this convincing proof, the authorities remain sceptical. They have dismissed photographic evidence of what are said to be plumbers at work in flooded lavatories as either 'a string of otters' or a 'floating mat of vegetation'.

Frenzied reports by over a dozen observers in Harwich last month that not one but *two* Water Board representatives hovered eerily outside a block of flats for nearly an hour, have been attributed to a meteorological balloon, or possibly Venus.

How long will it be before the Government tackles this frightening question? Dr. Maelström is urgently taking his case to a publisher, and believes he has enough evidence to convince anyone browsing through an airport bookstall.

Where have all the plumbers gone?

Fit from the neck up

Facial Yoga For All

In the hurly-burly of the eighties, increasing numbers of us have difficulty finding the time to take much physical exercise. As a result, more and more people are turning to the teachings of the Guru Moolah Swami Mazooma and his School Of Facial Yoga.

This remarkable art was developed by the Guru in Korea from a technique evolved over thousands of pounds of enrolment fees. It uses only the muscles of the part of the body above the tie, and can be practised anywhere with hardly any discomfort.

For that reason many leading public figures and politicians have been using it for

years. They find it tones up the cheek muscles, stimulates those lips and eyelids, and gives the rest of us a good laugh. Many believe that facial yoga can cure such occupational hazards as pendulous lips, receding chins, small shifty eyes and lumbago of the brain.

Facial Yoga can be practised by anyone. But be warned, watch out for sloppy (or worse, *dangerous*) misuse of the technique by so-called 'experts'.

Here our own Rowan Atkinson, himself a lifelong devotee of the Swami, puts right some commonly-seen mistakes.

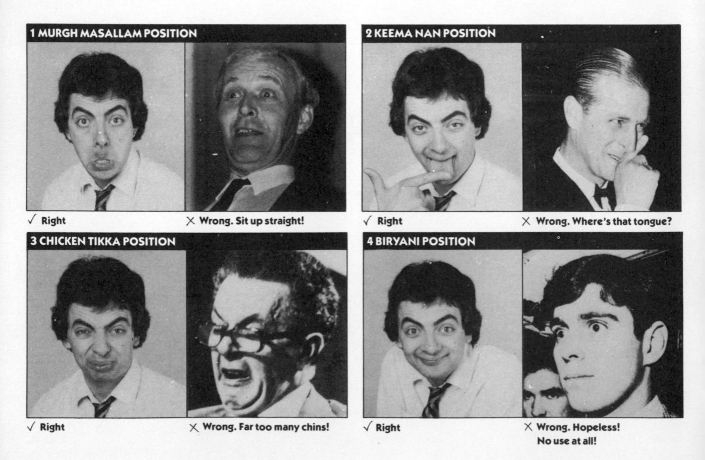

1 MURGH MASALLAM POSITION
✓ Right   ✗ Wrong. Sit up straight!

2 KEEMA NAN POSITION
✓ Right   ✗ Wrong. Where's that tongue?

3 CHICKEN TIKKA POSITION
✓ Right   ✗ Wrong. Far too many chins!

4 BIRYANI POSITION
✓ Right   ✗ Wrong. Hopeless!
No use at all!

5 BASMATI PILAO POSITION

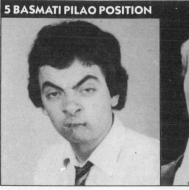 

✓ Right   ✗ **Wrong. Don't use the hands!**

6 ONION BHAJI POSITION

✓ Right   ✗ **Wrong. Call that a scowl?**

7 RAITA CHAPATI POSITION

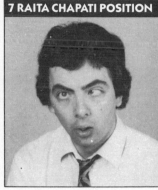 

✓ Right   ✗ **Wrong. The eyeballs must learn to do it without help!**

8 TWO-HALF LAGER POSITION

✓ Right   ✗ **Wrong. Biro far too prominent!**

The Listener Crossword 7,890,405

OVIDIAN
SET BY ATAHUALPA

The numbered squares are the cornerstones of an acrostical anti-clockwise cypher. Each down light must be anagrammatized before insertion, and those containing allusory or reticulated references to polymolecular unsaturated rhizomes must be set aside to await insertion in a NW-by-W direction, after being translitcrated phonetically into Iraqi patois, of the across lights. Remove the remaining across lights from the grid, and beat firmly with a stout elm or mahogany pargeter's coving tool until melded. Add the parsley choppings, the clove of garlic and nubbo (or Duke's swort) to taste. Garnish with anchovies. Serves 2. All words appear in Davidson's Lexicon of Ahami Badinage and Hen-tending Terms (York Press 1896).

1 As Niobe to the fleshpots. (6)
2 Coruscate 'daintily'. (5)
3 Bloke in Barchester? Not bloody likely. (7)
4 Whinnet-shaped so m'fellow has it. (9)
5 Sit old pogo rod on dim raffia newel-post. Hey nonny! (3, 1, 1, 29)
6 Inevitably, Tycho, you Brahe like a donkey. Or Mule, God wot. (2)
7 '…turning in the gyre' with malice aforethought? (8)

8 Quark-a-day. (4)
9 Notary-pokery, perhaps? (1, 7-12)
10-28 You have to make these up yourself, I'm not giving you any more clues. I've practically given it away already. (-Atahualpa)
29 Wastewater, says Thomas, and a', then turns to dubbin. (0)
30 Scud – the satrap loves him! (19)

Solution to Crossword 7,890,404

Prizewinners

Atahualpa
14, The Cuttings,
Maidenhead, Berks.

Mrs Atahualpa
14, The Cuttings,
Maidenhead, Berks.

Easy Crossword

CLUE ACROSS
1 Ninth letter of the alphabet.
CLUE DOWN
1 Visual organ, we hear.

Last Week's Solution

|¹A||

VIDEO TEASER

Getting it taped

Jeremy and Fiona decide to watch *Testament of Youth* on BBC2. Episode Two is about to start. Jeremy watched Episode One on transmission last week, and recorded it on his video cassette recorder for Fiona. She has not yet had time to see it. Jeremy wants to record *The Rockford Files* on BBC1 while he watches Episode Two of *Testament of Youth* on BBC2. Fiona wants to watch *The Krypton Factor* on ITV while she records Episode Two of *Testament of Youth*. Their neighbours, Anthony and Jenny, also have a video recorder, and have borrowed Jeremy and Fiona's tape of Episode One of *Testament of Youth*, which they plan to watch while recording *The Krypton Factor*. Their au pair wants to watch Part Three of *Life on Earth* on *her* machine: it starts on BBC-117 minutes before the end of *Testament of Youth*. Anthony and Jenny discover they only have enough space left on their tape to record the first 34 minutes of their programme. How will they all make out?

Answer on page 56.

❝ Are you a Gay Christian? If so, then that's fine by me. I don't mind at all. If homosexuality is 'your bag', if that's the kind of thing you're into - great. Fantastic. But don't be ashamed. Stand up Come 'out of the toilet' as the phrase has it. Say proudly 'I am tempted to be one'. You may even decide - after much prayer - to enter into a committed, even tempted, relationship with a member of the same genital group. And if you do, and if you feel you really can do nothing about it, you've been to a psychiatrist, had aversion therapy, tied metal weights to your private parts and *still* feel these tendencies, then I'm afraid it just means that God wants you to have a rotten life.

God's like that. He hates poofs.**❞**

GAY CHRISTIAN AID

Help us to find treasures on earth

"It is easier for a rich man to enter a camel, than it is for a poor man to." *Genitals III, viii*

SPACE INVADERS

SAUCER SCOOPS THE CUP

The ritual challenge match between Damon Webb and Del Harris was held again in the Saloon Bar of the Londis Arms, Harlow New Town, last Wednesday evening. Webb, the brilliant young Stevenage player, won the toss and kicked off as Player One, leaving Harris, more experienced but still one of the country's youngest Grand Bleeding Bloody Genius's, to bring up the rear. Webb settled for an unambitious but solid start, plumping for Mortimer's Opening, the old classic where the third row is demolished first, involving only one right-hand dodge before tackling row two, then swooping immediately back to the extreme left-hand row and clearing the ground for the first spaceship.

In this class of play, of course, all players are "shot-counters", knowing that you must hit the overhead beeper ship directly after the twenty second shot. Webb accomplished this in style, not only scoring the maximum 300 points, but going for Flash Harry's Kill – a neat jab to the Fire Button with the left elbow, ducking left for a quick drag on the fag in the ashtray placed *derrière-dessous* on the table, ordering and paying for two half-and-halfs and a pernod and blackcurrant and reaching back on his blind side to tackle Row 6 with the left ring-finger. A nice touch, not often seen these days outside of Tokyo.

Within minutes Webb had cleared his first deck, gained his extra shooter at 1500, and made some pretty stylish mincemeat of deck two. He caught his second squeaker (or "little last bugger that goes like the bloody clappers" as they say in local parlance) within millimetres of the top of the right-centre house. A lucky escape, but he went on to top 4,500 before a bad mistake cost him his first dead shooter.

Harris to play as Player Two. He began, as ever, with his thoughtful, almost languid, study of the board, reading the instructions carefully twice, observing his opponent carefully for signs of strain, and finally seeking out and hunting down with almost ruthless accuracy the fire button which he located first time, and gripped firmly beneath the famous Harris beaver-tail thumb. With superb control he eased his tank to the far right, making, with consummate aplomb, for Consuelo's Reverse, a new opening which demands taking the sixth row first. But Webb was too quick for him; anticipating his defeat in 7,800 moves' time he swung into the attack, plunging a Honda 250 camshaft needle up and into Harris's liver, dodging the falling corpse, leaping the plastic screen into the Snug Bar and committing adultery with Harris's wife in one of the auld-style nooks before going on to commit three daring Disco murders at El Cordobes in Toshack Street.

Another victory for Webb. Good to see him back on the old form.

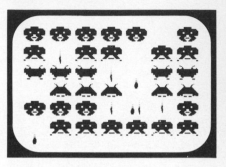

Problem this week

Player One to fire and win in three moves.

BRIDGE PROBLEM

What the hell is going on here?

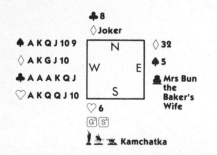

North and East discover that both have been marking the cards, using the symbols but with different meanings. West passes a spade with difficulty, swings his partner to the right and emerges to confront South eight miles to the East, from where his artillery can operate out of range of North's radar. Winds Southerly, Force 8.

Solution to Bridge Problem 234
Across the Bosphorous, joining Europe to Asia Minor with a single span of 4,389 feet.

CHESS PROBLEM

SET BY ATAHUALPA

White to play and win in ten down (anag.)

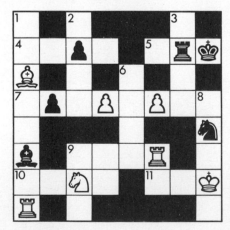

Heseltine's dilemma writ large – cut and run or let it all hang out! (Remember what happened to Boyson in last week's tussle with Sassoon). K9 to Q until set.

DK Djugashvili, our regular Chess Editor, is on holiday.

Video Teaser Answer

The au pair is Vietnamese, and cannot tell the difference between *Life On Earth* and *The Rockford Files,* which she watches next door with Jeremy while recording Episode Two of *Life On Earth.* Eventually they get bored and go to bed. Anthony and Jenny have a row. Jenny retires to the au pair's room and watches a tape of the previous Thursday's News while recording the second half of *The Rockford Files* which Jeremy sees the following day. Anthony goes down the pub. Fiona cannot work Anthony and Jenny's machine, and accidentally records Ceefax over their copy of *The Longest Day.*

NOT! STOP!! SHE BEGGED

BLOOD

The most precious commodity you have. Don't hoard it. Give it.
We need your blood now. Desperately. Give us your blood.
Every last drop of it. At once. We must have it.
Help us to help ourselves.

GIVE US YOUR BLOOD. GIVE GENEROUSLY. NOW.

This is an appeal on behalf of the four main clearing banks: Lloyds National Westminster Barclays and Midland.

Where else can you
get a hamburger
half way up the A37?

Travellers Fare 125

*This is the age of the spam

The Hole Truth...

'Self-portrait' (Lost, believed stolen) 1961

The artist Marcus Kellog was born in Beckenham, Kent, in 1935. He studied at the Royal College under Hepworth and has exhibited all over the world, most recently at last year's Milton Keynes Biennial. He describes his work as "a minimalist adjunct to Landscape" which strives towards a universal proletarian accessibility, abstracted from Newtonian concepts of Time and Space.

Marcus Kellog's greatest influence was undoubtedly Henry Moore. In the late fifties, he noticed that Moore's holes were getting bigger and bigger, while the amount of stone he used was getting correspondingly smaller and smaller. But Moore seemed reluctant to make the ultimate gesture: to dispense with the stone altogether, and just work with the holes. Kellog felt no such inhibitions. He got rid of all his stone, and used nothing but holes for his work.

"I'm afraid that, in retrospect, I can see that most of my early work tends to be just a pastiche of Henry's best holes. You don't have to look far to find the hole from 'Reclining Woman', or the void from 'Mother and Painful Swelling'."

'Empty Bath-Interior' (Private Collection of Peter Parker) 1969

He set about joining the holes up with anything he could lay his hands on: cavities from sponges, gruyère cheeses, ventilation bricks. But the end product still evolved inside a fundamentally representational concept: a case of the artist – as it were – painting what he doesn't see.

"There's a work of mine from that period in the foyer of Euston Station – you may know it, it's called 'Empty Bath – Interior', constructed primarily with the inside of spaghetti rings. A lot of people said to me, 'But that doesn't look like a bath!'. Then I suddenly realised what I was

doing. The essence of nihilistism. It came to me in a blinding mental block. And that is that people, in spite of what is staring them in the face, always see what they want to see. If they say it's a horse, then it's a horse, and not a bath. So that makes things easier for the artist." But not, presumably, for the jockey? "No, not for the jockey, I suppose. Not if he has to ride a bath in a race."

'Monument to the Unknown Cyclist' (Metropolitan Museum of Art) 1978

So Kellog abandoned titling his work, and kept quiet about his inspirations, although his obsession with holisticism continued. He found that the essence of isn'tness lent itself to anything from religious to contemporary themes – for example "A Policeman, If You Want One", which was inspired by the difference between Barry Manilow's songs, and his recent "View Through Politician's Head". But they're just starting points, and the final interpretation is in the eye of the beholder.

Two years ago, however, he started titling his work again.

Mobile: 'Space Between Two Rims' (Milton Keynes Leisure Centre) 1971

Recent Acquisitions

"I found that the public – except of course for Melvyn Bragg – couldn't see what I was trying to do. And I also realised that my holes and voids *could* have a quality of isness about them. 'Space Above A Plinth In A Park In London', for example. If I move it, it becomes 'A Different Space Above A Plinth', and so on."

Kellog's sculptures are not cheap: they're also expensive to insure, and vulnerable to theft. So who's going to buy them?

"Fools mostly. And the Arts Council. In fact anyone who wants the experience of having a bit of their sitting room actually *in* their sitting room."

ABOVE TOP: 'Self-portrait' by V Van Guard.
ABOVE: 'Incident on the Line' by Mondrian.

BUZBY

BOOKS

The Fourth Kennedy Brother
Clifford Irving
(Thin Books)
Is there a fourth Kennedy brother who's been going around bumping off the others so that he can have a crack at the Presidency? Irving thinks so.
Paperback. 12 pages. £5.25.

Is God A Conservative MP?
Dr. Conrad Maelström
(University of Stockholm Press)
Dr. Maelström argues convincingly that Sir Keith Joseph is in fact an android, cloned by an alien civilisation and planted on earth to bring about something beyond human understanding. The evidence, both medical and photographic, seems irrefutable. Includes an index of Sir Keith's principal design defects, and the full text of his speech to Blackpool Rotary Club.
224 pages. Illus. Price subj. to market forces.

The Vanishing Royals
Kenneth and Beatrice Matt.
(Health and Efficiency Press)
In the past, regal in-breeding has brought about the collapse of many dynasties, among them the Hanoverians (schizophrenia), the Hapsburgs (dropsy), the Tsars (haemophilia) and the Belgians (contagious boringness). Now a husband and wife team from the Rowse Institute has produced research which indicates that the present British Royal Family has contracted *regina nervosa,* a rare hereditary shrinking disease. To conceal their affliction from the public, Buckingham Palace has gone to enormous lengths to ensure that the Queen is only photographed in public with afflicted members of her own family and has arranged marriages with tiny commoners (Lord Snowdon, Mark Phillips). Other pointers: a high incidence of State Visits by midgets (King Hussein, Haile Selassie), strange choice of Birthday Honours (Ronnie Corbett, Arthur Askey, Lester Piggott), and veterinary evidence which suggests that the royal 'corgis' could in fact be a little known species of Brazilian hamster. (See photo).
2 vols. Illus. £21.25.

The Truth About The Police
Ken Lift and Glasgow Anarchists Commune
(Kremlin Publications)
Lift contends that the British Police behave the way they do because they're bitter about having gone deaf through years of having their sirens turned up painfully loud. In the limited space available here I will try to give away all the best bits in the book. If the police aren't deaf, argues Lift, why else do burglar alarms on shops ring night and day without anyone coming to investigate? Why do policemen say 'Look at me when I'm talking to you'? (How else can they lip-read?) Why are policemen getting younger every year? (A deliberate recruiting policy to find cadets who haven't gone deaf yet.) He explains how police interrogations escalate into violence; not hearing the answers to their questions they assume the accused 'won't talk' and try to beat it out of them. Then not knowing what the prisoner has actually said they have to go into court and make it up from guesswork. "He then said: 'It's a fair cop, guv', m'lud". The book includes a secret X-ray photograph of the inside of a police helmet showing the giant bulbous hearing aid stored there. Lift wants new legislation to prevent the police covering the head of the accused with blankets. He believes we may discover they have been amputating villains' ears for use in transplant experiments.
124 charts. 16 diagrams. £4.95.

NOT! BESTSELLERS*

1 **Diary of an Edwardian Literary Agent (0)**
(Maiden Aunt Books, £12.95)

2 **The Nigel Rees Book of Frank Muir Jokes About Stephen Pile by Giles Brandreth** (as told to Robert Morley) **(2½)**
(Rank Xerox Publications, £4.50)

3 **The Mitchell Beazley Enormous Book of Leaves (880)**
(Breadboard Books, £38.95)

4 **The AA Book of Free Sunglasses Pouch Offers (6)**
(Leaflet and Pedalbin, Send No Money Now)

5 **And Then the Butterfly Vomited** by David Niven **(124)**
(Maxwell House, £2.50)

6 **Inside The Queen Mother** by Tom Fleming **(12)**
(Horse & Bedroom Ltd., £16.50)

7 **Gibbons In My Duvet** by Dr Phyllis Meade **(36)**
(Penguin, £2.50)

8 **The Guinness Book of Drunks (5)**
(Cheese & Onion, £4.50)

9 **The Gourmet's Abattoir** by James Herriot/ Delia Smith **(40)**
(Harlech Afternoon Television Prodns., £7.95)

10 **The Nice Bible** by Cliff Richard/ Robert Dougal **(3)**
(Men Only, £0.22)

*****Figures in brackets show number of pages actually contributed by author himself without help from a parent or guardian or Bill Tidy cartoon.**

The Shrinking Royals. So small that four of them can now fit into one pram.

Esther Rantzen

calman

Nationwide

God, am I sick of the BBC! I am really so bloody bleeding effing bloody bored. Earlier tonight I saw bloody *Nationwide*. Now that is CRAP. God, how I hate that programme, it's so bloody banal! Pointless characterless commuter entertainment, I mean the people they bloody get on, I mean really *useful* people, you know, really valuable members of society, like people who can play Monopoly blindfold with one foot in the lavatory while they sing "Sergeant Pepper's Lonely Hearts Club Band", I mean really useful bloody skills — they're the sort of twats they have on *Nationwide*, y'know people who impersonate trombones. I mean what's the world coming to, that's the BB bloody C for you. And there's only one programme worse than *Nationwide* and that's that bloody *That's Life*: bleeding bloody Esther bleeding bloody effing bloody Rantzen bloody woman. They think they're so bloody important, they think they've got such a bloody social conscience, don't they? There's her swanning around in the foreground like an overgrown walking denture commercial and behind her there's that cross-eyed baboon who farts around in front of the bloody rubber plant and behind him there's those two nancy boys prissing about: I mean these people are *famous* for Christ's sakes! I mean what's happening to this bloody country? I'm going to get my licence fee back.
Eric Swannage,
Liverpool.

HUGH BREEM, Acting Head of Features Programmes, BBC TV, writes:
I'm glad Mr Swannage at least watches our programmes. What he omits to mention is that the item on board games for the tone deaf (Nationwide, March 12) *was part of a longer analysis of unemployment in Scotland. I can find no record of the trombonist-impersonator — could it be Ian Paisley (joke)?*

The Test Card

Well done the BBC! Another winner! The Test Card is quite magnificent: it justifies the Licence Fee on its own. Personally, I think the fee is far too low. I would willingly sell my house and all its contents to help the BBC!
E. Pitman
Camberwell

Controller, BBC 1, writes:
This is only one of over 85,000 letters we've received praising the Test Card. We hope to repeat it soon.

Just because Janet Street-Porter is married to Desmond Wilcox doesn't mean ITV have to pay her £200,000 a year to wander round the country sticking her teeth in where they're not wanted. You'd think that for that amount of money people could afford to go to the dentist once in a while!
Roger Jacobs
Norwich. (*£5 Letter)

Porn Again

If there's one programme on BBC that's worse than all the others it's *Are You Being Bloody Served,* with that buck-toothed queen, bloody Larry Grayson. I say Larry Grayson because I think Larry Grayson and John Inman are the same bloody person. You think about it. The BBC could be doing all their worst programmes on the cheap. Funnier things have happened. In fact a lot of funnier things have happened than *Are You Being Served.* Take this week's programme. There's Mr Humphrey's, or whoever he bloody is, stroking the cat belonging to Mrs Slocombe and the cat goes "miaow, miaow" and Mrs Slocombe turns to John bloody Inman/Larry bloody Grayson and says, "Mr Humphries, leave my pussy alone!" BBC family bloody entertainment indeed!
Richard Goodall
Halifax.

Larry Grayson

calman

Points of View

I think *Points of View* is a load of crap!
Terry Wallace
Cheam.

Barry Took writes:
I think you're a load of crap too, Mr Wallace!

Blake's Seven

calman

The Licence Fee

If the BBC's so bloody short of money, I've got some suggestions for the sort of people who could be taken off the payroll and sent off to fight World War Three:
For Starters: Bob Monkhouse.
Secondly: whoever it was thought up the idea for *Blake's Seven.*
Thirdly: anyone who laughs at Kenneth Robinson's jokes on *Start the Week.*
Fourthly: Bob bloody know-all Wilson.
Colin Baker
Belfast.

Controller, Finance, writes:
I'm afraid Mr Baker's suggestion would save the BBC less than he thinks, since Mr Monkhouse himself provided the inspiration for Blake's Seven, *and also owns the voice behind the appreciative laughter on* Start the Week. *But, yes, we're looking into the possibility of replacing Bob Wilson with a digital alarm clock snooze button.*

Who says the BBC wastes money? I wonder how many viewers have spotted the fact that Jan Leeming borrows all her frocks from the cast of *Blake's Seven*?
Maureen Francis
Torbay

Head of Costume writes:
Well spotted, Ms Francis! And did you know that Jan reads the news naked from the waist down?

NOT! VERY WELL HE GROWLED

WHAT'S ON

When to go, where do I begin, what to put on, why not wear that Laura Ashley thing, I know but who'll notice, how's your father, what's the time, who the hell's that at this hour, how should I know, whose idea was it in the first bloody place...

THEATRE GUIDE

Adelphi
Green Finger Exercise
Alan Ayckbourn's perennial hit, set in a suburban greenhouse. With Penelope Keith, Barry Foster, Dinsdale Landen, etc.

Ambassadors
Sofa And No Further
Revival of Alan Ayckbourn's smash, set in the conservatory of a suburban town hall. With Francis Matthews, Tessa Wyatt, Beryl Reid, etc.

Apollo
A Nice Safe Night Out
By Alan Ayckbourn, set in the garden furnishings department of a suburban store. With Peter Bowles, Fiona Richmond, Norman St John Stevas, etc.

Arts Theatre
Dental Mime Ensemble of Krakow
Last week. Recommended.

Brian Rix in My Suspenders is Killing Me!

Comedy Theatre
Side by Side By Sandie Shaw
Robin Ray recreates musical magic from the career of the bare-foot Dagenham waif. With Rita Webb.

Cambridge
Tommy Steele in Hamlet by William Shakespeare. West End transfer of the Sheffield Crucible production, with Marti Caine, Giant Haystacks, Ralph Richardson.

Criterion
Scurvy!
Lionel Bart's vivacious family musical, based on the childhood of General Booth. With Una Stubbs, John Howard Davies.

Alan Ayckbourn's Lesbian Lavatory Lust

Duchess
A Bus Load Of WI's
By Alan Ayckbourn. Comedy of misunderstandings set in a bank-manager's potting shed. With Derek Nimmo, Leslie Phillips, Julia McKenzie.

Duke of York's
Les Parapluies De Zimbabwe
Tim Rice/Andrew Lloyd Webber musical about the late President Vorster's love of cats.

Garrick
My Suspenders Is Killing Me!
With Brian Rix.

Hampstead
Bum Fart Willie
By Billy Connolly, directed by Ken Campbell for the Tiny Theatre Behind The Gents At The Bunch Of Grapes Company.

Haymarket
Lesbian Lavatory Lust
By Alan Ayckbourn. Two paedophiles on the rampage in pre-war Hamburg. Colour. 96 minutes.

Lyric Theatre
Sophistries
By Tom Stoppard

Royal Court
Toe
By Samuel Beckett. The author himself directs in darkness.

St Martins
Agatha Christie's *The Policeman Did It*. 37th Hyperbolic Billing.

Nowhere To Park, Very Long Queues For The Cloakroom, And Don't Forget To Tip The Gorilla On The Door Or He'll Drop Your Fox Fur In The Gutter Theatre
The Swingin' Blue Jeans
Toy with a wimpy in noisy and uncomfortable surroundings while thousands of overweight chorus girls and sequinned nancy boys dance over your handbag. Tickets from £65.

CINEMA GUIDE

ABC 1, 2, 3, 4, 5, 6, 7, 8, 9, & 14
Leicester Square

11 **The Empire Falls Flat (U)**
12 **Everything You Always Hated About Woody Allen But Never Dared Admit (X)**
13 **American Relish Tray (X)**
14 **Mangez Mon Croissant**

('They Eat Horses, Don't They?') (X) Hilarious romp with two gay French Chefs.

CERTIFICATE
U This is to certify that
JACKANORY, THE MOVIE
has been passed by
Lord Harlech

Odeon
Marble Arch

Walt Disney's **Jim-Jam Cases and Flip-Flops (U)**
2 **Timmy's Puppy (U)**
3 **The Wonderful World Of The Hyena (U)**
4 **When Eight-Year Olds Drop 'Em (U)**

CERTIFICATE
U This is to certify that
WILLY WONKA AND THE CHOCOLATE FACTORY
has been passed by
Lord Harlech

The Smelly Little Hut Up The Alley
Ladbroke Grove

Where Nurses Shove It (X)
Male Emanuelle IV Does It With Chickens (X)

CERTIFICATE
X This is to certify that
LESBIAN LAVATORY LUST
has been passed by

RESTAURANTS
by Milo Barnes
Ventricles, 34, Transit Ave, Birmingham 48.

Ventricles, the new non-vegetarian bistro, is strictly for carnivores and people who hate cruelty to vegetables. At dinner last week, I plumped for the 'Chicken Kiev' (the outside of a chicken, stuffed with the inside of a chicken, nestling in a bed of fluffy white lice), while my companion chose the Roast Beef and Yorkshire. The beef was delicious, but the Terrier was perhaps a trifle gamey. Non-vegetables range from Green Purple-Sprouting Rabbit Insides, Pea-Sized Bits of Donkey, and Things Rather like Onions. I preferred not to ask what exactly they were. Salads are offered in profusion: Grey, Dark Brown Hairy, Dappled and Feathered, Palomino With Hooves, but no Green Salads just now, as parrots are out of season.

The Wine Butcher persuaded us to try Bulls Blood, but you can also have the house giraffe (either red or white corpuscles). Dinner from around £55.50, but they also do a splendid businessman's breakfast (pig slices and two unborn children of a hen) for much less.

WORST SELLERS

1 *The Blue Peter Book of Cheating:* a guide to passing exams. (BBC Publications) £70.
2 *Let's Learn To Swim The Teddy Kennedy Way* – James Earl Carter (Pentagon Press) $8.40.
3 *Reach for the Handrail* – Douglas Bader (More Tat About A War That Finished 35 Years Ago Press) £3.95.
4 The Reader's Digest *Complete Abridged But Still Very Long Labour Cabinet Ministers Bitchy Remarks About Each Other 1964-70* – Tony Benn, Barbara Castle, Michael Foot, Richard Crossman, Harold Wilson (Small Fortune Press) £235.90.
5 *A Frogman's Guide to Venice* (Time Life) Great Crumbling Cities of the World Series £6.90.

Undressed To Kill – at the Plaza from Monday. 104 Minutes. Nude Kung-fu Maniac slaughters thousands of innocent Christmas shoppers while waiting to be connected to Directory Enquiries.

CLASSIFIED

● SENSITIVE TOLERANT Piscean woman, mid-twenties, interested travel, antiques, long walks, wishes to meet shy, humorous, caring, non-smoking male for bondage, discipline, TV etc. No cranks please, Box 342.

● SAVE THE WHALE urgently needs sympathetic swimming pool owners. Will deliver. Phone Clare on 4491 ex 56.

● RESEARCHER working for leading TV Consumer Programme urgently requires undertakers whose names rhyme with 'bottom', 'organ', 'fletcher'. Write in confidence c/o That's Life! BBC TV London W12.

● DO YOU WANT YOUR BRAIN REMOVED? Church of the 13th Coming (Marxist-Leninist). Courses for young people at The Grange, Aylett's Cross, Nr Crawley. Electro-therapy, sensory deprivation, very little to eat. In three weeks you'll think you can levitate. A chance to earn brown rice portions by selling rotten LPs to passers-by in Oxford Street. Free dust-cover uniform and haircut. Send sae for introductory pamphlet which conclusively disproves Darwinism, gravity, etc, plus cheque for £650 to: Rev Ho Vis, The Grange, Aylett's Cross.

● FEMALE CONSCIOUSNESS-LOWERING GROUPS. Therapy sessions with qualified divorce lawyer. Rediscover bits of your body which disgust you, how to sell your bicycle etc. Box 67.

● EVES YEAST AND YOGURT DINER 3b, Camden High Street, Bsmt. 'Hot Tubs of Soya'. Live kitchen theatre. Eve and her waitresses use space and time to share an expressionistic experience in movement using only their internal organs. First folio (in praise of the adulki bean) is unmissable. For the initial twenty minutes Eve and her women sit soaking in a large basin of water, but in the final moments Eve expands. Lindsey Tull. £1 + meal. Women only.

● EXHIBITION National Theatre. All week. Another of the National's adventurous summer seasons. An 80ft egg has been placed on the roof, with a 200ft chicken on top of it, exploring the theme of 'Which goes first – the chicken, the egg or the National Theatre?'. If you missed last month's pilchard in the Upper Circle at the Aldwych – don't miss this.

● RATS AHOY – Liftshaft Theatre, Battersea. A new musical comedy based on the Black Plague. Monopedes welcome. 8.00. £1.50.

● OKLAHOMA! Under Arches, Albert Bridge. The Bruce House dossers present this tough, no-nonsense family classic. Go, if only for the explosive rendering of 'Oh What A Beautiful Morning!', a nail-biting camp-fire sequence, featuring the Paraffin Addicts Chorus. £1.15. Free, Bring a bottle.

● ANTI-VEGETARIAN MARCH, Thursday 12.00, Berni Inn Piccadilly to Berni Inn Hounslow. Meat-lovers! Join this back-to-the-flesh campaign for those who feel that vegetarianism leads to a boring society full of pathetic little weeds who wear shoes with heels at the front. Trouble last week broke out when a piece of bacon was forced between a counter-demonstrator's rissoles, and panic ensued when a hoaxer rang up and claimed to have planted a pork chop in the building. In the scuffles that followed a pig (supporting the anti-vegetarian cause) was seriously eaten. However this week's march has been promised army protection.

A LIFE IN THE DAY OF

COLONEL GADDAFI

 Allah guides my breakfast — normally paprika and a glass of humus. Then I read the Koran looking for loopholes until my brain aches. Then I do something deranged, have supper, and go to bed.

NOT!

NEXT WEEK!

By next week some idiot in your house will have thrown this magazine away mistaking it for a colour supplement. You will have to buy another copy next week, and in it you can look forward to seeing this page again.

Cruft's: Best Bitch 1980

Feature: It was in rusting, elderly, ill-equipped vessels such as these that the Hammersmith Bus People began their journey of hope. Many of them have paid up to 57p to travel in conditions of appalling discomfort. Read their horrifying story in next week's issue.

CROYDON SHOOTS 600 BUS PEOPLE – 'Plenty more room on top now' says Councillor.

Medicine: The cloning of General Dayan

NOT! (CONT. ON PAGE 1)